The Essential Rules for
Bar Exam Success

By

Steven I. Friedland
Professor of Law
Elon University School of Law

with

Jeffrey Scott Shapiro, Esq.

THOMSON

™

WEST

Mat #40544200

© 2008 Thomson/West
      610 Opperman Drive
      St. Paul, MN 55123
      1–800–313–9378

Printed in the United States of America

ISBN: 978–0–314–17678–3

 *TEXT IS PRINTED ON 10% POST CONSUMER RECYCLED PAPER*

PREFACE

The Essential Rules for Bar Exam Success may seem like a strange name for a book whose subject is to teach you what you supposedly already learned in three long years of law school. But let's face it, how many times did your professors stop in Contracts class and say, "Now that I've explained that consideration is a bargained for exchange, let me take an extra moment to tell you how to apply it on the bar exam." If your professor is like most professors, they probably never said anything like that at all.

The point of our title is that the bar exam is different than law school in a lot of ways. It has its own set of very distinguishable rules, obstacles and wording. It is almost safe to say that the National Conference of Bar Examiners (NCBE), the folks who write the Multistate Bar Exam (MBE), incorporate a writing style that comes right out of the Restatement, the U.C.C. and the Federal Rules of Evidence. In their own peculiar way, the bar examiners are an unknown entity to most law students. Not many law students know much about why they pick the answer choices they do, but we're going to do our best in this book to help get you acquainted.

Now, don't get too excited. This book isn't a 'magic pill' that's going to make the pain, drudgery and required effort disappear into the horizon. After all, you've got to put in your due diligence. Preparation isn't merely about input (meaning how many bar courses you can take or how many materials you're using); it's also about output (what you learn from those materials).

If that sounds simple, try this on for size - many people delude themselves into thinking that if they've done 2000 practice questions they're going to pass with flying colors. Okay, maybe you did 2000 questions, but did you get them right? And, if you got them right do you know why you got them right? Do you understand why the wrong answers are *wrong*? If you can't answer yes to all of the preceding questions, you're not learning; you're guessing to a certain extent, and that's going to usually take you to one place, the front door of Lady Luck.

Now, let us tell you a little about our friend, Lady Luck, since she isn't often that kind to bar takers. It isn't uncommon for people to miss their state limit by anywhere from 1 to 5 points, and if you're on the edge, you often will come close but not close enough. It's rarely the reverse – barely passing – when gambling with the bar exam.

Confused? Don't worry. We're going to explain all of this later on. Just do yourself a favor right now and take this advice – don't find out how the examiners do things the hard way. Let's get this right the first time. If you're taking this exam for the second time, then let's make sure there's not a third. And if you're taking it for the umpteenth time, let's make this your last. You can do it. Just believe in yourself and avoid the mistake of studying the wrong way. If you already have, it's time to unlearn it. Remember, no matter how far you've gone down the wrong road, you still have to turn back to get on the right road. You need two months or more to effectively prepare for the bar exam. We're going to get into time management in a few pages. You've already made the first move by reading this book, so sit back, relax and take it all in.

ACKNOWLEDGEMENTS

With thanks and appreciation to: my wife, Jennifer, for her unflagging support; my children for taking me away from this project whenever they show up in front of me; my parents, for their concern and interest in all that I do; my sister and brothers, who I can always count on; Jane Law, who should be named Jane Terrific, for her professional and helpful administrative assistance with the many versions of this manuscript; my research assistants, Danielle Caldwell, Seemah Shaw and Eleftherios Xixis, who, while mentioned later in a brief note, deserve mention again for their ruthless persistence in their reviews of the book; and finally, my grandparents, particularly Ethel and Rose, who I recognize more and more each day as trailblazers, paving the way for my generation.

Steven I. Friedland

~ ~ ~

With deep gratitude to Brooke, for the incredible love, care and compassion she has given me throughout the years and for the wonderful times we have shared together; great appreciation to my mother, father, sister, cousins and good friend, Jeff Woodward, for their unrelenting belief in me; unforgettable thanks to Scott Bauries and Angela Brayer for their selfless tutoring and support during law school at the University of Florida; additional thanks to fellow Gators Dave Benjamin, Derrick Valkenburg, Taylor Kessel, Ryan Mitchell, Tim Anderson, Norm Bledsoe, Alex Mestagh, Annika Davidson, Joann Guerrero, Autumn Miller, Trisha Mason and Colette Duke; respect for Professors Traci Rambo, Lyrissa Lidsky, Steve Greenberg, Jennifer Zedalis and Jeffrey Morton; a wave of sympathy for Dan Dickenson, Dave Benn, Hillel Presser and

Acknowledgements

Andrea Reid for sticking it out with me during the bar exam until the bitter, yet rewarding end; indebtedness to CBS News producers Susan Zirinsky, Joe Halderman, Doug Longhini, Erin Moriarity and Al Briganti, Journal News editors John Alcott and Bill Falk as well as my Section Chief, Duane Kokesch at the Washington, D.C. Attorney General's Office for teaching me the respective trades of journalism and law. Finally, a very special thanks to former Boulder District Attorney Alex Hunter, former Boulder Detective Steve Thomas and especially, First Amendment crusader Professor Rod Smolla, for inspiring me to go to law school and make a difference in the world.

Jeffrey Scott Shapiro

ABOUT THE AUTHORS

Professor Steven I. Friedland has been a full-time professor of law for more than 20 years at several different law schools, currently as a Professor and Senior Scholar at Elon University School of Law. Friedland has worked for more than a decade with students who have had difficulty passing the bar exam. An honors graduate of Binghamton University and Harvard Law School, he also holds LL.M. and J.S.D. degrees from Columbia University. A former Assistant U.S. Attorney in Washington, D.C., Friedland has written several Evidence Law textbooks, a student guide to Criminal Law and a Constitutional Law textbook. He can be reached at: *sfriedland2@elon.edu*.

Jeffrey Scott Shapiro is a nationally recognized investigative journalist who graduated from the University of Florida Levin School of Law in 2005 and was sworn in to practice law in Florida in 2006. Jeff specializes in covering high-profile criminal cases and writes columns about political and legal affairs. Jeff is now prosecuting criminal cases for the Office of the Attorney General for the District of Columbia. He can be reached at his online site at: *http://drinkthis.typepad.com/shapiro/*.

A NOTE FROM STEVEN I. FRIEDLAND

This book had several sources of inspiration. It is partly based on educational literature about learning. It's also founded on a compilation of personal experiences, from teaching full-time in law schools for 20 years, to teaching bar review courses for more than a decade, to taking and passing three states' bar exams and, perhaps most importantly, to tutoring many students after they failed the bar exam on multiple occasions. This book draws significantly from the experiences of many students who have passed – and failed – the exam. All these sources have taught me that not everyone learns the same way, especially when it comes to the very unforgiving bar exam. Consequently, this book has been designed to offer a variety of techniques and strategies, especially for those people who have difficulty in preparing for and succeeding on a test of the magnitude and nature of the bar exam.

While the book had many sources of inspiration, it also had many sources of preparation. In addition to Jeffrey Shapiro's way with words, I owe a debt of gratitude to the capable assistance of Jane Law, Danielle Caldwell, Seema Shah and Eleftherios Xixis.

Because the essence of this book is about preparing efficiently, and not simply about the number of total hours logged, it is filled with pragmatic tips to help make good use of your true bar prep currency: TIME. In a sense, this book is your navigational guide through foreign land – namely the bar exam. Take it from us, it is a land you will visit once – and hope to never see again. We hope it guides you well.

A NOTE FROM JEFFREY SCOTT SHAPIRO

Okay, you've just graduated from law school, but instead of taking off to Hawaii or Europe for a vacation, you're forced to endure one of the hardest challenges of your life. That may sound disappointing, but don't despair.

When I graduated from law school at the University of Florida in May 2005, I only had a week before my first bar preparation class began with PMBR. A few days after that was over, I started my other bar prep class with BARBRI. It's unfortunate that I didn't get in the study mode the first couple of weeks, because once I did, I was learning more than I ever have. The hardest part was actually not knowing how much I had to study and how to make use of my time effectively.

As time went on, I realized that although the BARBRI prep class schedule was a good barometer on how to spend my time, I needed to really adapt to my own study needs. Instead of moving forward as the schedule dictated, I eventually started studying what I needed to, the way I needed to learn it best. This proved to be much more effective.

When I first met Professor Friedland, it was during a tutoring session at a small Fort Lauderdale-based coffee shop only a mile from the Florida beaches. It was difficult to keep my mind off of the fact that it was warm outside and what I really wanted to do was go surfing. Instead, I focused and did what had to be done. Friedland introduced a methodology that, surprisingly, I had never learned in law school. However, it was what I had been *looking for* and that's because it's what every law student craves - organization and assertive technique to break down problems into black letter law. In this book, we cut to the chase. We don't give you a 'magic pill' on how to pass, but we are going to give you some solid advice on how to study so you can make this as painless as possible. We're also going to cover some hot MBE areas and break them down for you so you have a head start.

Unlike my co-author, I was never a 'book-smart' student. Professor Friedland graduated with honors from Harvard Law, taught evidence at University of Miami fresh out of law school and quickly landed a job as a federal prosecutor. I, on the other hand, practically earned straight C's my first semester in law school. By the time I graduated, however, I achieved Magna Cum Laude status my final semester and received the "Book Award" in Trial Practice. Like many of you reading this now, I was a late starter.

When I studied for the bar exam, I started out very unsure of how to proceed. If I had known how to study correctly from the first day, I would have had a much easier time with it. Whatever kind of student you are, you can channel your particular strengths in a creative way to pass this exam.

I strongly suggest you use the methods in this book and stay in close contact with your classmates whether they're from law school or a bar prep class, if they're studying as effectively as you are. Not only will their feedback be helpful in learning course material, it will help keep you going. Don't get down. You're about to learn more about the law in a few weeks than you learned in all three years of law school. If you had any doubt in your mind about your knowledge of the law, you'll know it by exam time. Remember, although this test is important, it's not life or death. Try to keep it in perspective. This is simply a rite of passage, nothing more. If the bar examiners were 'cool,' it would be a straightforward test. But the bar examiners are definitely not cool, not in the least. They're going to try and throw you off course. We're going to keep you on it. Whether you're taking this test for the first time or the third time, play it cool, play it smart and keep your head held high. You'll come out of this alive and maybe even with a license to practice law.

PROLOGUE

Gilda Radner, the comedienne, used to rant on *Saturday Night Live* as the character Rosanne Roseannadanna, "If it isn't one thing, it's another." People who have difficulty with the bar exam usually attribute it to one thing or another. Those reasons fall along a broad spectrum, ranging from a lack of mental preparation, to an unwillingness to devote the necessary time and effort, to bad test-taking skills. For some people, the long and winding bar exam road leads to a plethora of motivational problems. For others, the surprise comes when they finally 'get' that they really had no idea how to study properly. This book was designed to help people who are hurt by "one thing or another" by offering some ideas of how to approach the test effectively. Since people learn differently, we're going to offer you a few different strategies to choose from.

We are going to focus on the three most important things you will need to pass the bar exam: (1) Course and question frameworks (a.k.a. maps); (2) Deep knowledge; and (3) Application (transferring your knowledge to different fact patterns and contexts).

Even if this book helps you minimize, but not eliminate, preparation mistakes, it should still be of value. Although the goal of preparation is mastery and you should plan on an Air Force strategy (aiming high), your real objective is just to pass. Remember, this is not law school. First lesson - you don't need an "A" on this exam. You just need to get a C$^+$. Don't exhaust yourself cramming in every tiny detail. Learn the "big rocks," the "main courses," the essential rules of the bar exam. Don't worry so much about the "side salads," at least not yet. Prioritize – some things are indeed more important than others.

Most students pass the bar exam on the first try, so don't worry. This test is far from impossible. With the guidance of a few touchstones, including structure, discipline, mastery of the essential material and competency in critical reading, thinking and writing under time pressure, you can pass the bar exam and move on with your life. Or, you can go back to having a life. Now that we've set the record straight, let's get on with it.

TABLE OF CONTENTS

Table of Contents

Table of Contents

Table of Contents

Table of Contents

Table of Contents

Table of Contents

I. <u>INTRODUCTION</u>

Chapter Points:
(1) Be Prepared.
(2) Don't Get Down.

Some Important Points:
(1) The Bar Exam is Different than Law School.
(2) Prepare for the Worst, Hope for the Best.
(3) Say, "Yes I Can."

A. ONE CRUEL TRICK

In some ways, the bar exam is the cruelest trick of all. After three years of law school, a steady diet of legal rules and principles, and countless hours spent reading casebooks, you finally get to walk across the graduation stage. In front of cheering family and friends, you are handed your diploma and for that brief moment you feel as if the long journey to become a lawyer is finally over. Instead, the march to glory across the graduation stage is a short-lived mirage. It's really just a warm up for a 6-week marathon preparing for the bar exam.

Now, you knew all along that there was going to be a bar exam, but it had always been a distant mountain. But now that mountain is right in front of you and the sample questions look a lot different than what you thought. With the bar exam mountain looming overhead, let's face it - you're bummed out.

B. BAR PREP BLUES

At a recent law school graduation ceremony, I ran across a highly successful student named Elena. Elena was pretty excited as she walked across the stage and happily hugged her family and friends. If anyone could handle the bar prep stresses, everyone figured, it was Elena. Yet, just two weeks later, she couldn't have been further removed from her former self, wearing what seemed to be a permanent frown, as she tried to dig herself out of the bar prep blues. By the time of the exam, she was worn out, unsmiling and just plain tired – exhausted from studying, sick of the subject matter and fed up with the singular demands of the bar exam. The long and short of it was that she wasn't mentally and emotionally prepared to take the exam and she didn't pass. Don't get the bar prep blues – psyche yourself up. You're about to experience one of the hardest processes of your life. However, if you truly have a curiosity about the law and want to tie up some of those loose ends you never really got in law school - it could be one of the great experiences of your life. You're going to be amazed how smart you really are and, little by little, you're going to notice yourself advance and progress.

C. WHAT MAKES THE BAR EXAM SO TOUGH?

> *"It is good to go into the bar prep period understanding that preparing for the bar exam is not supposed to be easy."*

Why is the bar exam so frustrating, even for the most accomplished of students like Elena? There are a lot of reasons, ranging from the organizational to the psychological. The main reason is that there are numerous distinctions between the bar exam and traditional law school finals. Let's start with a few distinctions to get this point across before it's too late.

1. *No Real Professor*

In law school, you probably heard the old saying, "you take the teacher, not the course," meaning, each professor had a particular way of teaching a course, so that how the material was delivered was more important than the material itself. Throughout the semester, you had the chance to pick up on the little nuances of what that professor liked and didn't like and you had a pretty good idea of how to impress him or her come exam time. On the bar exam, there is no such teacher and no clues about what the bar exam "teacher" emphasizes and prioritizes on the exam. Instead, students are expected to know all of the pertinent rules with equal depth and completeness, regardless of what the agenda was in the comparable law school class. In fact, you'll get a pretty good idea once you begin studying for the bar exam which of your professors did you a favor by teaching the right material and which ones taught what they wanted.

2. No Casebooks

In law school, casebooks often dictate the nature of the course and its coverage. If you took the time to read them, you knew that the teacher often assigned only one case in an area and that the depth of coverage often was much less than if the teacher assigned several cases on the same rule. Thus, the depth of analysis and expectations of the professor varied significantly from topic to topic and professor to professor. No such variation exists for the bar exam. You are expected to understand all of the legal rules in depth and then to be able to apply them. It's a one-shot deal, and you either learn it the right way or you don't. We're going to make sure you learn it the right way.

3. No Loose Requirements of Conciseness and Precision

With multiple hour essay exams in law school, students often could get away with being a bit wordy (or a lot wordy) and offering additional information (a.k.a. "the note dump"). Because of the time pressure, law professors also sometimes discounted a lack of precision or polish in the responses. The multiple choice questions on the bar examination aren't nearly as forgiving, particularly when you've only got 1.8 minutes to sort out several areas of law in a single question.

4. No Accompanying Law School Course

Unlike law school exams, appended to the end of a semester of related classes, the two-month preparation for the bar examination is entirely free-standing, without any classes at all – unless one counts the bar review courses, which are not really "courses" at all, but rather a series of distinct lectures about substantive law. Yes, all lectures. It almost makes you miss getting called on. Nonetheless, you can't get away with playing spider solitaire or instant messaging in the bar review classes because they're essentially a "knowledge dump" of information and every second counts. Bar review courses have no attendance or preparation requirement, generally no professors answering or asking questions and no assignments with responsive feedback. Much like the first year of college, you'll first find the lack of oversight liberating. The freedom is a double-edged sword, though, allowing you to relax your motivation and discipline until it is too late.

5. No Total Focus on Issue-Spotter Essays

The bar exam also could be called "the revenge of the standardized test," given its emphasis on multiple choice item types. For those students who enjoyed the refuge of law school from the predominance of multiple choice questions, you're going to hate it. Clear and simple, you're going to hate it. Accept it, get it out of your system and get used to it, because we're going to get you to love it. Once you start getting these questions right and you figure out the methodology, don't be surprised if you welcome the challenge. After all, the Multistate Bar Exam alone is composed of 200 multiple choice questions and many state components have multiple choice questions as well as essay items. It's time to get used to them.

6. *No Essays Containing a "Discuss" Call of the Question*

In law school exams, professors untrained in the science of test creation often ask students to simply "discuss" the legal issues in the fact patterns, conditioning students to provide a general analysis of a topic, even throwing in all of their notes. You probably became good at answering those types of questions. Of course, that's not the way the bar examiners ask the questions, which are much more precise and call for narrowly guided responses. It's about attorney competence now – not law student competence. Those used to padding an answer may be very surprised that effect does not work on the bar exam. It becomes a tough lesson – the bar exam is a different game.

7. *Supersized: Not Just One Course at a Time*

The bar exam is a "supersized" test, covering a multitude of subjects without labels, and it can overwhelm you psychologically and physically. For the first time, questions in evidence law, property law, constitutional law, and more can be asked back to back to back – as well as on the state portions of the exam, even to the extent that federal and state questions are mixed together in the same essay. You may get a contracts question where a lawyer will transfer money from a client's retainer into the lawyer's personal account. Regardless of what state you live in, this should raise alarm bells.

The novelty of questions not being limited to one course subject can raise your anxiety levels to heights not felt since the first year of law school. Quite simply, it's going to freak you out a little. Furthermore, the exam becomes an endurance contest, the likes of which students have not experienced in their three years of legal training (or anywhere else). The "tons" of material can wear on students in such a way that it leads to a pessimistic and eventual self-fulfilling prophesy of failure, throwing students off balance. Irrational behavior may result – from waterproofing the books to get extra study time in the shower to keeping books open in the car to study while at traffic lights. Don't get crazy. Just be cool. Take the time and learn what you're reading.

8. *It's All-or-Nothing: No Easy Electives to Balance the Schedule*

Finally, there is the specter of failure. If you don't pass this test, you're probably worried that you'll never become a lawyer. In Wisconsin, you're breathing easy. If you've graduated from a Wisconsin law school, you don't have to pass the bar exam to practice law there. However, that's not the rule anywhere else, so you're not alone in those fears. (Although note that Virginia has an apprenticeship rule, New Hampshire just started an alternative bar certificate program, and other states have special rules for schools within their states.) The specter of failure and the "all-or-nothing" nature of the test weighs heavily on even the most successful of law students. For many students, passing the test is necessary to maintain current or future employment. Let's face it - no one wants to lose his or her job. If you've already secured one, you probably don't want to lose yours either. Not only is it counter-productive, it's a little embarrassing. For others, the months of singular focus simply heighten the tension about the apparent fine line between admission to the profession and rejection. For nearly everyone, those law school loans will require repayment soon (yikes), and repayment will be nearly impossible without a decent salary. Okay, so how do you avoid all of this? First: Take a deep breath. Now dig in. And remember: it is not brain surgery. If you look through the Yellow Pages, there are plenty of attorneys who made it through – somehow. Relax. You're going to do just fine.

"When you get discouraged, just check the Yellow Pages under the listing "attorneys." Look at all of the pictures.
If they can survive the bar exam, so can you."

II. FAMILIARITY WITH THE BAR EXAM

Chapter Points:
(1) Understanding Multiple Choice Questions.
(2) Understanding Essays.

A. THE TEST ON PAPER – THE MULTISTATE EXAM

Ironically, because the bar exam is a different type of test than those that preceded it, you're going to be in uncharted waters – just like being first year students all over again. Gee, aren't you lucky? Getting the edge on bar exam preparation requires understanding the bar exam "game" just as much as law school exams offered a "game" or undergraduate evaluations provided a "game." For some students, the lack of understanding about the "game" coincides with the lack of a "game plan."

Most bar examinations are two or three days long. Florida has only a two-day exam whereas California and New York, states that include performance testing, have a three-day exam. Question types vary. Although most bar examinations rely heavily on objective questions, such as multiple choice, essays are still an important component.

The Multistate Bar Exam consists of 200 multiple choice questions divided equally into morning and afternoon sessions, each lasting three hours. There are six subjects tested: Torts, Criminal Law and Procedure, Constitutional Law, Contracts, Property Law, and Evidence. Each of the subjects has roughly the same number of questions (33) and the questions are mixed up, meaning they're not divided by courses one at a time.

The Bar Examiners have started pre-testing some questions. This means some of the 200 questions do not count. Since you do not know which of the questions do not count, you

7

have to treat all of the questions the same. In February 2007, apparently 10 of the 200 questions were pre-tested.

The National Conference of Bar Examiners publicly discloses which topics within the courses are going to be the most highly tested. In fact, you'd be wise to take a look at their web site at www.ncbex.com. Check out some of their practice questions (there's a free downloadable booklet) and even consider ordering some of their older MBE tests. They've released three exams from 1991 through 1998 and have released additional questions in recent years. Get familiar with the language, the font and the style that the examiners like to use. Just don't become too dependent on all of the answers in those older tests. Remember, in some areas, like Constitutional Law or Criminal Procedure, the law has changed over time. In other more traditional areas, like Property, the law and the nature of the responses most likely will be the same.

> *"Emphasize in your studies what the bar examiners will emphasize on the test."*

1. Some Highly Tested Topics (See, e.g., the National Conference of Bar Examiners, "Most Highly Tested Topics by Course" 2005.)

Constitutional Law
Individual rights matter a lot. These range from Equal Protection, to Due Process, to the Privileges and Immunities Clause to, of course, the First Amendment.

Criminal Law & Procedure
While everyone focuses on common law crimes, such as criminal homicide, it is important to know search and seizure issues from the Fourth Amendment as well as *Miranda* issues from the Fifth Amendment and right to counsel issues from the Sixth Amendment.

Contracts

In contracts, everyone reacts most viscerally to third party beneficiary questions. The most tested, though, are basic formation issues. Conditions and remedies also matter.

Evidence

In questions about Evidence, both law school courses and the bar exam are in sync, focusing on hearsay. The vast expanse of hearsay, however, requires knowledge of what out-of-court assertions are not hearsay, as well as what statements fall within the exceptions. And what about the dreaded Best Evidence Rule? It is on the exam, but not a highlight for the examiners.

Property

Property law covers a wide variety of subjects and often feels like a fantastically fast road-trip through ten countries in five days. While basic Property concepts, such as easements, covenants, adverse possession, estates in land and future interests, are covered, the examiners have taken a liking to mortgages in recent years. For many students, mortgages were not even included in their basic courses.

Torts

Like Torts in law school, Torts on the bar exam emphasizes negligence. Of course negligence comes in many shapes and hues, including negligence per se, res ipsa loquitur and differing standards of care.

2. Scoring

Okay, it's not just what's on the bar exam that matters, but how those questions are scored as well. There's no penalty for answering questions incorrectly, so if you really don't know the answer, just go for it and take your best shot. You've got nothing to lose, so make sure you don't leave a single answer blank. The raw score, meaning the number of questions you actually answer correctly, is scaled (their term for curved) to equate the difficulty of the test with other MBE exams. They are concerned about uniformity. You are concerned about doing well.

Here's the tricky part. There's no easy way to figure out the curve (which is usually between 10-15 points) because the worse you do, the higher your curve is. The examiners also subjectively take into account the difficulty level of each exam. According to the MBE Information Booklet:

> "A statistical process called equating adjusts for variations in the difficulty of different forms of the examination so that any particular scaled score will represent the same level of performance from test to test. For instance, if a test were more difficult than previous tests, then the scaled scores on that test would be adjusted upward to account for this difference. The purpose of these adjustments is to help ensure that no applicant is unfairly penalized (or rewarded) for taking a more (or less) difficult form of the test."[1]

In addition to the examiners taking the difficulty level of each exam into account, they also will scale your score based on how well you do. The better all of the test-takers do, the lower the curve will be. Don't even ask. It's very complicated and it's a waste of time to worry about it. Try going over the rules for damages in Contracts instead of trying to figure out the NCBE scaling formula. Just assume you'll get a few extra points, but don't count on them. Got it? Let's keep going.

---

[1] *The MBE 2006 Information Booklet*, National Conference of Bar Examiners, (2005).

> Scoring is complicated. But it should not hide one fact – your goal should be to answer everything. Completion is Step #1.

B. THE STATE COMPONENTS

The state component of the bar examination lasts one to two days. It may consist of various question types, from multiple choice to essays, to performance testing, in which students are given a carefully designed "case library" and asked to answer questions about a hypothetical scenario that is based on a particular topic. The state exam components often focus on essay writing, but might include other forms of questions, such as multiple choice item types. A growing number of states are using performance testing.

1. Essay Questions

The essay questions on the bar examination are based on a variety of subjects. Many states test a larger number of subjects than others and essays can mix together several subjects or be solely committed to a single topic. In Arizona, for example, there are no multiple choice questions on its state bar exam. Instead, there are a dozen essays. When essay questions are given, they are usually offered in a uniform manner, with the same length of time allotted and the same approach to legal issues. The essays are distinctive, however, when compared to essay questions on law school exams. The calls of bar exam essay questions often are very specific and directed. Rarely will a bar exam question be framed as "Discuss" or "Analyze the legal issues." There also may be two or more questions asked in a single essay. Remember, this isn't law school. Don't expect the expected.

> Get ready for essay questions that have specific directives for their questions asked, not just the common law school request, "Discuss."

2. Multiple Choice Questions

The state component of the multiple choice tests can differ significantly from the Multistate Exam. The state multiple choice item types may have a wider set of goals than the Multistate – testing such things as simple knowledge of the rules, understanding of the elements, issue spotting and problem solving. The state multiple choice questions may parallel the Multistate question, and might confound students when the state distinction is that there is none. Remember, some state laws will mirror the common law pretty closely, so if you end up in one of these states, you're in luck. Just don't count on it. If you master the common law for the Multistate, the state distinctions shouldn't be too hard to remember.

3. Performance Testing

Performance testing is designed to resemble a mock "case file," including a set of facts, a law "library" and a specific directive for the respondent. While it's not exactly a simulation of lawyering, it is much more of an approximation of lawyering than multiple choice questions or essay items under time pressure. These types of questions have their own common themes and flow, and test-takers should become familiar with them.

C. THE BASICS OF MULTIPLE CHOICE AND ESSAY QUESTIONS

1. Dissecting Multiple Choice Type Questions

A major component of the exam involves multiple choice type questions, which must be answered under considerable time pressure. Almost all states have adopted the multistate examination, comprised of 200 multiple choice questions administered in two three-hour segments, one segment in the morning and one in the afternoon after a lunch break. There is no penalty for wrong answers and the test is scaled based on its difficulty. The questions cover six major substantive areas – Evidence, Criminal Law and Procedure, Torts, Contracts, Constitutional Law and Property.

> *Multiple choice questions include several significant parts – the stimulus, the stem, options and the key.*

2. Components

There are several components of multiple choice questions. These include (1) the stimulus, (2) the stem of the question, (3) options and (4) the key. The *stimulus,* or body of the question, comprises the brief hypothetical or fact pattern needed to answer the question. The *stem* of the question, or call, provides the inquiry or legal question about the stimulus. The *options*, or answer choices, follow the stimulus and stem. Of the options, three are usually incorrect, incomplete or irrelevant for one reason or another and one is the *key* or best answer. However, sometimes, there appears to be more than one technically correct answer. That is why the examiners want you to choose the best answer. No one said it would be easy - but you'll figure it out.

Unlike law school essays, the question stimulus in multiple choice questions is much more compact and tailored to fit specific needs. This does not mean, however, that the legal issue is any more obvious than in law school issue spotters. The stimulus (body of the question) provides the context and facts needed to answer the call of the question (the question itself). Critical reading of the stimulus is crucial to answering each question.

The stem or call of the question can take a variety of forms. Unlike law school issue spotters, which may be general and incomplete, the stem is usually a complete sentence and stocked with important clues about the question. The stem is very important in multiple choice questions and, therefore, should be read with care. Here are some of the common ones:

a. **Sample Stems:**
1. The <u>best/worst argument</u> by a Plaintiff is....
2. Defendant should argue... Defendant should not argue...
3. The <u>most likely outcome</u> to the problem is.... (*i.e.,* who will likely prevail on the legal issue)
4. If Plaintiff wins or Plaintiff loses it will most likely be because...

b. **Stem Tasks:**
1. Identify the applicable area of law that matters (or for that matter, why?).
2. Which element of the rule applies?
3. What does the element mean?
4. This illustrates which rule?
5. Does the rule apply - OR does an exception?
6. Compare this rule to another.

Okay, got all that? Don't worry. We're just getting acquainted with the format. It's going to take a little bit of time to get familiar with all of this. Once you do some practice questions and finish this book, you'll have these formats down like the back of your hand.

Wrong answer choices generally fall within the "3 i's" – incorrect, incomplete or irrelevant

---

The next component of multiple choice questions is the options, better known as answer choices. (We're going to repeat ourselves from time to time to hammer this into you. Just take it in.)

Options generally possess a similar structure, length and amount of detail to minimize guessing. The best option or key should be MORE than marginally better than the incorrect choices – although it will seem on many of the questions that there are two very good choices. Incorrect answer choices generally should fall within the "3 i's:" *incorrect, incomplete, or irrelevant.*

> Example of the "3 i's"
> A grants B the right to walk across A's land from B's adjacent property "for B's lifetime." One year later, A puts up a "no trespassing" sign and a very high fence, yelling at B, "Don't walk across my land anymore!" If B sues A for the right to walk across A's land, will B win?
>
> A. A wins because B was given an easement in gross. (incorrect)
> B. A wins if B had notice A was walking on B's land every other day. (irrelevant)
> C. B wins if A's grant was in writing. (best choice, reflecting an important characteristic of an easement)
> D. B wins if B relied on A's grant to B's detriment. (incomplete)

A is incorrect because the type of interest B received relates to A's land as well. Therefore, the easement is "appurtenant" to A's land and is not an easement in gross. The particular fact mentioned in B concerning use of the servient property and whether there is notice is irrelevant. The "notice" issue arises when determining whether an easement runs with the land and binds successor-owners. It is irrelevant to determine whether A's initial grant "for B's lifetime" is valid. One fact in answer choice D is helpful but not dispositive - whether B relied on A's promise. This estoppel argument is incomplete, however, because there is no indication whether the reliance was reasonable. The element of reasonableness is necessary for answer choice D to be correct. The best answer choice, consequently, likely will be C because it states an important component of a valid conveyance of an interest in land, that it generally must be in writing.

3. *Three Primary Multiple Choice Question Types*

There are three common multiple choice question types. Perhaps the most widely used is the basic duality – two answer choices stating one conclusion and two answer choices stating another conclusion. (*i.e.,* (A) Yes ..., (B) Yes ..., (C) No ..., (D) No....) You're going to be faced with four options (although three can be successfully used as well) and rarely, if ever, will see a "none of the above" choice. That is because the creators of the question want you to analyze each answer choice, not guess that somewhere in the "none of the above" universe there exists a preferable answer.

While some of the options may have similar conclusions, each of the four options are distinguished. For example, there may be different rationales contained in each option.

Who will win, A or B?

A. A wins because of fact X.
B. A wins because of fact Y.
C. B wins because of legal doctrine Z.
D. B wins because of legal doctrine AA.

The Multiple-Multiple

Another common question type is the compound, or "multiple-multiple" question. This question form allows the question creator to offer more than one correct response. The reader must discern which are the best answer choices and why.

For example:

> Why will A most likely win?
>
> I. A has a good defense.
> II. The Court lacks jurisdiction.
> III. B violated the Statute of Limitations.
>
> A. I only.
> B. I and II.
> C. I, II and III.
> D. I and III.

The Series

A third common question type is the series question, which most closely approximates the essay, if only because several questions share a single fact pattern. (If no questions were asked, it would approximate an "issue spotter" essay.) You're going to be asked to respond to several different types of questions about the same set of facts. A series question generally starts when the students are told, for example, "Questions 1-3 are based on the following facts . . ." The questions may be related or may deal with different rules or subject areas. Be ready and keep your focus and don't forget the original set of facts. This question type brings in the skill of recall more than the other types. Don't hesitate to refer back to the fact pattern if you must because it could mean the difference in analyzing an answer choice correctly or incorrectly.

4. Dissecting Essay Questions

Perhaps the greatest distinction between law school essay exams and the bar exam is the way the questions are asked. Bar examiners usually have very specific, directed "stems" – the part of the question in which the test-taker is asked to do something. In law school, many of the exams simply ask the students to "discuss the legal issues presented" or even just "discuss." On the bar exam, the questions usually are in complete sentences and often ask the students to play a particular role, like an attorney for a defendant.

The specific nature of the stems throw off some students who answer them in the same way they did in law school. However, the specific orientation of the stem often transforms the question and you may miss out on responding to the specific question that was actually asked.

Another distinction is that while bar essays often are "issue spotters," they are not "overstuffed" with more issues than the time allows. Law school tempts students to skim and skirt the primary topics. It is not second nature to some, but you should get down to business with the issues you see. Read and answer carefully and thoroughly, especially with your analysis.

Now, before you go on, make sure you know the following:

1. The meaning of the word "stimulus."
2. The meaning of the word "stem."
3. The meaning of the word "option."

Got it? Good! **<u>TAKE A BREAK</u>**. You've earned it!

III. <u>COMMON MISTAKES BAR-TAKERS MAKE</u>

Chapter Points:
(1) Study Techniques Matter.
(2) Reading, Not Skimming, is Critical.
(3) Time Management Also Matters a Lot.

Some Important Points:
(1) People who Fail the Bar often Make Similar Mistakes.
(2) Without Feedback, Some People Who Fail Never See it Coming.

There are plenty of reasons why students don't pass the bar exam. Most of the time, it has nothing to do with how intelligent they are. It has more to do with the choices they make between the time they should start studying and the time they take the exam. Taking the bar exam is different than any other exam most students have ever taken and that's because it is written in its own vocabulary, almost like a secret code. Your objective is to decrypt that code and feel comfortable when taking the exam so you don't get intimidated or upset when you stumble across a word or question that seems confusing.

There will always be a few people who have a natural propensity for taking this test. You know whom we're talking about – those folks from law school who aced every class and never stressed or panicked. Chances are that if you're reading this book, you're not one of them. But don't worry because most of us aren't. Don't let those kinds of people get you down because by the time you've finished this book, if you've done what we've told you, you're going to be in a position to pass this exam with confidence. Now, before we reveal our deepest, darkest secrets on how to pass the bar exam, we're going to tell you how to fail it. Pay close attention to this chapter because if you want to make sure you don't pass the bar exam – this is what you have to do.

OKAY, **READY**? *Here we go.*

A. NOT STUDYING

There are too many excuses for not studying, and they are rarely valid.

This isn't really a hard one, is it? If you don't study, you won't pass. But wait a minute. You didn't study to the bone in law school and you got away with passing, so maybe that'll work on the bar exam, right? No – wrong, *dead wrong*. In fact, if we had to bet, our money is on the likelihood that the bar examiners will be just fine if some of you fail – we'll tell you why later on. Here are some common thoughts people have when trying to justify the fact they're not studying as much as they should.

1. *"I can always take it again."*

Okay, don't be *this* person. You're looking at the bar exam as a practice test. You say, "It's just a way to familiarize myself with the process and the second time, I'll be in good shape to pass." Not a good move. It's understandable that you're nervous – and if you were never a great student, this approach may give you a sense of security because you're not putting too much pressure on yourself the first time around. We understand, but we don't recommend this way of thinking. The study process is intense and very exhausting. Take it from us. Once you've done it, you won't want to do it again. Plus, the second time around won't be a whole lot easier because the second exam will still be a lot different than the first one. Your objective should be simple. You're going to pass this thing the first time and put it behind you like it's a big black cloud receding on the horizon. Relax – you can do it.

2. *"I'm not sure if I'm going to practice law."*

Hold on – you went to law school, right? If you didn't go to practice law, what was the point? Maybe you were thinking it was a good way to pass the time, postpone getting a job and live off student loans? No, no, no - you're thinking of *graduate school*. This was *law school* for crying out loud. You worked really, really hard. Don't cheat yourself out of the privilege to have one of the most amazing powers in the world – the ability to walk into a courtroom and make a case for anyone you want. It's better to try and get the license now than wait and find out you'd prefer to have it down the road. Besides, there isn't an employer in the world that doesn't value an employee with a law license. You never know when it may help you get a promotion or a special opportunity. Plus, you may want to represent yourself one day, and although you don't *need* a law license, it offers a lot more credibility to have one than if you don't.

3. *"I'm just not motivated."*

Wait a minute; you mean you're *not* excited about studying the law all day and night? Okay, let's get real. *No one* wants to do this. (Okay, almost no one; there are always exceptions.) It's sort of the way you felt about your early morning or late afternoon Civil Procedure class. You didn't want to go and listen to that 12(b)(6) stuff either, but you did it, right? Of course you did. You wouldn't have graduated if you didn't.

Look, you already did the hard part. You paid your dues and served your three years in law school. Now you've just got to get excited about the fact that in two months, this could all be over forever! That's right – *forever*. Keep that in mind. Two months of studying may seem like a long time, but take it from us – it'll fly by, and before you know it, you'll be a few days away from countdown.

Once you start studying, you may notice a strange phenomenon occur. You're going to want to make sure you keep studying. It's almost like training for the Olympics. Once you've started to taste some success on your practice questions, you'll welcome the challenge and enjoy it. You'll also welcome the experience of discovering where your true strengths and weaknesses lie. You may surprise yourself and discover that what you thought you were bad at, you're actually good at. This is the real thing and it can be exciting if you stop dreading it and instead, just do it. Once you start, you may not be able to stop.

Sound impossible? *Watch and see.* Later, we'll brag that we told you so.

4. *"I am the master of the universe!"*

> *Remember what they say about pride leading to a fall?*
> *That saying also applies to the bar exam.*

Okay, so you were brilliant in law school – and in college and even elementary school. You were that person who aced every class and got elected to every important position. Congratulations. Okay, you may be smart, and you may be a great test-taker. However, as we said before, the bar exam uses a different testing style and vocabulary than your law school exams did and we're willing to bet that you're going to be unpleasantly surprised at how strange some of the questions may seem or why the answers are what they are.

If you need a little additional convincing, try *this one* on for size. **There are usually *two* appealing answers for every question, maybe even three or four!** Don't get excited, however, because you only get credit for *one.* That's right. The examiners aren't necessarily looking for a *right* answer. They want the *best* answer. You may be close, but close only counts in horseshoes and slow dancing. How will you know how to think like a bar examiner?

You'll know because we're going to show you. *Stick around.*

5. *"My family and friends need attention."*

Most friends and family will probably understand that the bar exam prep period is the equivalent of Olympics training for a law school graduate. You need time to get prepared and study and it's important that everyone knows the next couple of months are not going to be business as usual. Your friends, if they're cool, will get the picture that you can't go out partying because you have to keep that head clear and your family will have to know that sometimes the First Amendment may demand more time than expected, causing you delays for dinner and other planned events. If your friends don't get this, well, then you've got to ask yourself how much of a friend they really are. If your family needs your help, that's another story. If you've got children or a spouse in need, you will have to do the best you can to balance your home life with studying by letting everyone know that their help means a lot to you. Let them know that their understanding is just as important a part of your journey as your learning the material. Make them feel like they're a little part of a group effort because they are!

B. LETTING TIME SLIP AWAY

1. *Wasting Precious Time*

This is a great tactic if you want to fail. Unlike the popular 60s song, time is *not* on your side. How you spend your study time will mean the difference between passing and failing. If you study right, you'll make the most out of it and learn enough in half the time. That will allow you to focus carefully on the time you're taking to really study as opposed to pretending to study while multi-tasking and not retaining the information.

You have three choices. You can (1) waste your study time, (2) marginalize your study time or (3) really study for a solid block of time and succeed. Obviously, the first two options are not preferred. How do you achieve the third? It is not simply discipline. Focus on the areas that will substantially help you on the actual test, develop your test-taking skills under time pressure, and emphasize and go for deep understanding of the subject matter, using techniques that results show are the most helpful.

Another important mantra to follow is that it's important to focus. There's no point in wasting precious study time if you're just going to daydream or glaze over the material. "Seat time" does not count. It's much better to study hard for a while and then reward yourself with some real free time that you can enjoy. Don't be that student who reads the same passage hour after hour but feels guilty taking a break because they haven't really made any progress. Take a break and get it out of your system. Come back to the material when you're ready.

Finally, it may go without saying, but we're assuming you're smart enough not to procrastinate. Most of you will be taking a bar preparation course, or even two, during this process and you should use that class as a guide to where your studying should be. That doesn't mean your class should dictate everything you do. We define studying as learning. If you are not learning, you are not studying. This is especially true with material you find particularly difficult. It's more important to spend a lengthy block of time learning something you don't understand but need to understand than simply moving from one subject to the next because you're following a schedule.

2. *Substituting the Main Course for Side Salads*

This main course idea is important, so we've got a little test for you. You've just ordered dinner and, after much anticipation, your server finally comes out with what you ordered - a medium rare, juicy prime rib with mashed potatoes, creamed spinach and a side salad. Do you dig into the prime rib, or do you nibble at the salad and the vegetables first? If you're a nibbler, it's time to change your eating habits (or in this case, your study habits - don't worry you can still nibble at dinner, we won't mind). The prime rib represents the substance of the material you need to know - like understanding character evidence and impeachment or contract formation and damages. The side items are the little extra points like judicial notice and the parol evidence rule. You're not going to pass this exam by trying to digest a lot of little side items. You need to understand how to cook, eat and digest that prime rib and get to the main course first. Those side items are tempting, but take it from us – you'll feel so much better once you've gotten the prime rib out of the way and you can reward yourself with a brownie for dessert.

Law school does a great job of teaching you how to read cases, but it rarely teaches you how to study for a hard multi-subject exam. Most students don't really know how to study correctly or even take notes in class (and this means you, the student who was playing "Minesweeper" on your laptop or instant messaging your friends in the middle of Evidence class). Law school also fails to show students how to outline correctly by reorganizing their class notes into a hierarchy of points and how to synthesize material into coherent doctrines. We're going to show you how to do that.

3. *Location, Location, Location: Finding a Place to Go to Work*

The place where you study is important, but some people don't pay much attention to it. If you've somehow mastered the ability to study at home and it works for you, that's great. However, if you're like most of us, studying at home presents a wide array of problems. For starters, you never really know when your day has begun or ended. You may wake up, read an outline, make some breakfast and watch the *Today Show*. Then, you may try a practice run of questions and finally break for a shower. The phone will ring – you have to explain to your Mom how to cut and paste something on her PC since she doesn't really get it and by the time you get off the phone you're wondering, "Isn't it time for lunch?"

Hey! Don't let this happen to you. You've got a job to do and you'd better treat it like one. Get outta there! You'll do much better and you'll feel better if you choose a place to study and treat it like a regular job. Many students like to use study areas at big bookstores, libraries and even nearby universities or quiet coffeehouses. Plan on being there at a certain time, taking lunch and quitting at a certain time (unless you're on a roll). You can stay longer if you want, but the most important thing is making sure you start the day right - and that means getting to work on time.

One way to keep you motivated is to find another student or two who also wants to go to the same place. You don't have to study together, but it is good to know there's someone expecting you to be at work every day. It makes it harder to slack off. After all, a racehorse only runs as fast as his competition. If you know your friend is going to shoot you that disapproving look when you walk in an hour later to study Trusts, you're going to be more inclined to hustle. No one wants to feel like he or she copped out and you won't either. Make it a little tough on yourself and keep one another honest. It'll be good for both of you.

C. WORKING WHILE STUDYING

Working while preparing for the bar exam is common and sometimes unavoidable. With money being a scarce resource, it is a fact of life that bar exam preparations must coexist with having some source of income. Many students successfully negotiate jobs in combination with bar exam preparation, but it does ratchet up the level of difficulty. While lawyer-employers certainly understand the pressures and necessities of the bar exam, lawyers unfortunately seem to forget how much time is *really* needed to pass. The immediate demands of clients and cases cause lawyers to authorize weeks rather than months for studying – and that's an underestimation of what's needed.

It's not only the time spent working that causes problems, but also the way the time spent at work distracts students. Often, students who work full-time are very tired by the time they sit down to study. At the very least, they're distracted by ongoing cases and other office matters, diminishing the effectiveness of their studies.

Steve says:

A few years ago, while sitting in my office, I received a phone call from a former student named Todd. After a brief hesitation, Todd declared he had just flunked the bar. Todd was very smart and did very well in law school, so it was a bit surprising. But upon a closer look, it was not very surprising at all. In law school, Todd worked full-time and was not all that prepared for class. Instead, Todd cranked it up for exams. Todd sought advice on how he could improve his chances for the upcoming bar exam. Before I responded to his question, I asked him what had gone wrong. Finally, the obvious came out - Todd admitted he was working full-time throughout the bar prep period and that he didn't really have a chance to seriously study until a week and a half before the actual exam. I could almost see Todd's sheepish grin on the phone when he said, "Well, I know I need to study more. I was hoping to pull it out in the end just like in law school. I was too busy with my job, trying not to leave too many loose ends. I suppose I need to clear the necessary room in my schedule." The real reason for Todd's call was how to study effectively over time – without cramming. We had a good conversation, and each of us learned a thing or two. I received a call several months later, a day after bar results were made public. Todd kind of laughed, and I instantly knew what he had to say. He had passed – with plenty of points to spare.

Jeff Says:

Look, here's the thing. If you've got generous relatives, now is the time for them to help out. If not, think about taking out a bar exam loan. That's right! There are private loans available for law school graduates studying to take the bar exam, and they're very similar to student loans with similar interest rates and payment plans. You can easily get up to $15,000 if you need it. Be smart. Chances are you already owe tens of thousands of dollars for law school. The extra money needed to study for the bar exam will be worth it if it helps you pass.

D. ADOPTING A PASSIVE STUDYING APPROACH

Reading outlines is NOT the dominant preparation method that will generally help you pass the exam. If you prioritize this way, you might not be prepared for a test of questions – and not a mind-numbing number of rules. You can read hundreds, if not thousands, of rules over and over and although it will help you to some extent, it's not the bread and butter of a useful strategy. Instead, as they say in the military, you need a good tactical plan.

1. Making the Connection Between Reading and Applying

Reading the outlines usually helps more <u>after</u> you've had a chance to slip and fall on a few practice questions. For instance, you just finished a set of Criminal Law questions and you've discovered that you missed all 3 questions about conspiracy. After reading the answers you may be tempted to refer to your outlines and really dig in to what the rules for conspiracy are. The outlines are there to help you "fix" your knowledge as much as they are there to help you learn rules in the first place. Then, you'll take a serious interest in what you're reading because you'll be able to APPLY it to something you're actually working on.

It's not passive reading – it's active because you're taking an authentic interest in what you're reading. Remember, there's more than just reading. There are other cognitive operations you have to engage in like issue spotting, problem solving and evaluating answer choices.

Reading is like watching sports or others play a musical instrument. Performance is a far cry from observation. If you want to join in on a jam session, you've got to pick up that 6-string and start learning major chords – instead of just listening and playing an air guitar.

2. *The Wrong Kind of Reading*

Remember, on the bar exam, you're not going to simply be reading information passively and taking it in. You're going to have to aggressively tackle a multiple choice question and scan carefully for issues and exceptions. It's a different kind of reading than reading course materials or outlines.

3. *Digesting and Comprehending*

Like we said before, you can sometimes read the same passage or subject for hours, but if you're not absorbing it, you're not getting anywhere. Before you know it, the rules become a blur and you start mixing them up with one another. You're "in the soup." This is extremely common for nearly all bar takers and you need to be aware of it. It's almost like visiting 23 European countries in 3 days. You remember drinking a pint of Guinness with a team of rugby players in a cool little town tavern, but was that in London? Madrid? Dublin? They're all good candidates, but only one of them is the right answer. On the exam, you've got to get the right answer, and take it from us, many of them will all look the same.

4. Reading for the Wrong Reasons

Don't read to avoid practice questions. First of all, let's just level with you here. Practice questions are actually more fun. No, really, they are. Practice questions are challenging and engage the user in a game-like atmosphere where you're actively participating. Reading endless outlines is like taking a lengthy road trip on the Interstate. You keep passing the same kinds of trees and, every other rest stop has a Waffle House or a McDonald's. You'll find yourself getting very, very bored and asking yourself, "Are we there yet?"

5. Illustration: Training for a Marathon

When people enter a competitive race, such as the New York City Marathon, they train for the race by jogging regularly. Taking notes at a road-running lecture or watching a film on road racing might assist the runners in understanding the running process and their own form, but it's not the same as just getting out there and running. Only in preparing for the bar examination, it seems, do students predominantly - sometimes almost exclusively - watch tapes and listen to lecturers, rather than emphasizing the performance skills of writing essays and answering selected response items under time pressure. While the lecture/reading options might be helpful, they are a poor substitute for simulating the performance in question. The student has created an ineffective hierarchy of studying, with passive observation at the top of the hierarchy. Translation? Don't just read about the law; apply the law by practicing questions. Just do it!

E. SKIMMING THE RULES AND PRINCIPLES

1. A Skimmer's Approach to Reading and Understanding the Rules

A *skimmer* knows a little bit about a lot of rules, usually without precision, conciseness or depth. A useful illustration involves the famous Torts concept that every law student studies in his or her first year of school – *res ipsa loquitur*. Most skimmers remember something about res ipsa. If asked, the skimmers will say that res ipsa means "the thing speaks for itself." Unfortunately, that knowledge is almost worthless on the bar exam. In fact, you're almost better off not knowing anything than knowing only a little bit. Why? Because that's the kind of "knowledge" that will lead you to what we call a "sucker answer."

Here's a thought: you come back from lunch on exam day. You've had a really good sandwich and you're relaxed. You're a little tired and not too excited about another set of 100 multistate questions. You open up the second part of the MBE and ("oh, yes!") it's an easy Torts question. You look upwards and quietly think, "Thanks." It's a negligence problem and it's obvious that that the answer is . . . aha! There it is, *"Res Ipsa Loquitur!"*

Guess what. WRONG! Remember a "sucker answer" can look painfully obvious but lack one important element to make it correct. That's the kind of response the examiners can't wait to try out on you. A little bit of knowledge is dangerous. Here's what usually happens with skimmers:

The skimmer can't state what a phrase means or what the exact elements of *res ipsa* are, such as "the inference of negligence, exclusive control by the defendant, causation and damages." "Skimmers" abandon the mastery of the rules required to effectively answer highly focused bar exam questions. Instead, skimmers substitute guessing at some level of the analysis in lieu of thorough knowledge and understanding.

> *What good is memorizing a rule if you don't really know what it means?*

The skimmers are under the huge misconception that their approach to the rules equates to learning, when it often falls woefully short of the "deep knowledge" mastery required for the exam. These students are not aware of the depth of knowledge required to answer bar-type questions. These students believe victory comes to those who cover the most rules. Their overriding goal is quantity, not quality, from lectures to reading to problems to whatever format will cover a subject. They read every page of every bar review book in their possession – twice just to feel better than the guy sitting next to them in class. They learn the ins and outs of equity, even if it has not been tested in 15 years, and ask about a law overturned two years earlier – just in case.

2.   Illustration: Tommy the Skimmer at the "All-U-Can-Eat" Bar Book Buffet

Tommy twice took and failed the bar exam. He was disappointed because he had studied hard, setting out for the library when it opened and leaving it long after sunset, six days a week for several months. He wondered what went wrong. Yet when asked to describe the elements of burglary or an easement or third party beneficiary rights to a contract, he could not state them with accuracy or precision. Res ipsa loquitur was still "the thing speaks for itself," a generality that didn't actually help in *answering* a bar exam question. Even after he had studied the subjects again, he still could not, with precision, describe the elements of burglary and what they meant. Finally, the diagnosis had come into focus: Tommy wasn't really digesting the rules as he devoured them, so his mastery levels were quite low. Tommy tried to cover as much as he could, like at an all-u-can eat buffet, but all he was getting was an upset stomach. Tommy was used to skimming through the rules and absorbing them only generally, enough to get by. To pass the bar exam, Tommy had to start all over, not simply learning the substantive material, but first, how to study and absorb the material. Tommy first had to fully capture the material. Then it was retention, retention, and more retention. It was like learning to walk all over again. The skimming that had served Tommy well in law school – at least well enough to pass with a respectable grade point average – was now causing him to come up short on the bar exam. And he didn't know which way to turn.

The skimming strategy creates another problem – a failure to focus on exceptions to the rule, in addition to the rule itself. *When* exceptions apply is always a very significant question asked by the bar examiners. For example, while many persons review the Statute of Frauds in preparing for the bar, not as many people learn the exceptions to the Statute of Frauds – all those instances when a contract can be enforceable despite not being reduced to a writing. The failure to "go deep" and learn every-thing about a rule, especially its exceptions, is often what hurts folks because that is what the bar examiners are looking for. If you don't know them, you're not going to pass.

Learning the rules really means understanding the rules in-depth. Can you teach the rules to others like an expert?

F. OVER-STUDYING

Another symptom of studying incorrectly is challenging oneself the WRONG way. This is pretty common for very intelligent people. They think that more is better - the more questions they can do, whether they're learning the rule or not, or the more outlines they can read, whether they're really getting it or not, is going to help them. You need to remember something. Bigger isn't better and more isn't either.

The bar exam should not be treated like an "all you can eat" buffet that you hit during hazing week with a college fraternity to see who could eat the most. Instead, you should be the selective, careful eaters who are watching their diets. There's only so much you can digest (as we explained above) and you want to watch your calories so you don't eat too much. What happens to people who eat too much? Well, they get sick and then throw up. That doesn't do anyone any good. It's better to focus on a few solid rules per day and master them with full, easy digestion than stuff yourself with twice the amount of rules and get yourself dazed and confused.

1. Illustration: Danni, the Queen of Coverage

Danni sat through every minute of her bar review lecture and read all of the bar review books containing black letter law. She even took her books with her on vacation and continued to study the rules, including some topics that are rarely tested. Like many honor students, Danni believed that the old, conservative method of studying everything was paramount. Although Danni was studying constantly, she realized she could not recite too many rules with absolute precision. She also was starting to confuse the main rules with their exceptions and, even worse, the main exceptions tested with some of the more esoteric exceptions the bar examiners hardly ever test. For example, one day Danni devoted three whole hours to studying water law and distinguishing the difference between the famous common enemy rule with the less common prior appropriation rule and its even more unique California distinction known as the collateral rights doctrine. By the end of her study session, Danni had covered every area of water law.

There were only two problems. One, there's only one question at the most on water law on the bar exam and the exam answer is typically a basic one, which you can learn in about five minutes. Two, by the end of the day, she was starting to confuse the doctrines with one another. She had spent so much time studying so many different things about water law that they were all starting to blend together. Like a red rubber ball, the rules were starting to bounce right off of her instead of being absorbed by her. What you're going to learn about the bar exam is that only one thing really matters – how much you absorb, not cover.

> It's what you absorb, not cover,
> that really matters.

G. LETTING NEGATIVITY GET THE BEST OF YOU

Don't bum out. ALL of you are eventually going to start feeling negative about this exam. Some people, though, let negativity get in their way. It's extremely rare that someone marches into the bar exam with a jovial bounce and a big smile thinking about how excited they are to be there. No one wants to be there! Let's get real. You're all in the same boat and the fact of the matter is that the majority of you are going to pass. It's natural to feel nervous. Nerves are "as natural as granola." It's normal to feel like you haven't done enough when exam day comes around. Don't let it get to you. What's important is that you don't talk yourself out of passing the exam.

Here's why it's so important not to focus on your fears. It takes away from your concentration level to study. It also hurts your confidence. Confidence can lead you to the right answer. A lack of confidence? That will lead you to the wrong answer.

1. Illustration: The Allure of the Unknown

Rick had studied pretty hard for the bar exam but didn't feel quite satisfied when he walked in to take the Multistate. As he was going through questions he noticed some answers that looked kind of familiar and some that did not. In fact, some of the answers were Latin phrases he'd never even heard of, let alone knew thoroughly. Rick's logic was that since he didn't study as hard he could have, he must have missed a few things. If he missed some things and there were some doctrines or

35

phrases he didn't recognize or understand, then those answers must be the right answers. So Rick chose everything he did not know. WRONG! Those are generally the wrong answers.

Whether you realize it or not, if you've gone to class and done a substantial amount of questions, you've studied enough to recognize which answers are potentially right and which ones are totally out in left field. Would you order something in a restaurant that you've never heard of? You probably wouldn't. Don't do it on the bar exam either. It's much safer to give yourself the benefit of the doubt and stick with the salmon than to jump to something more exotic that you've never heard of.

2. *Quick Tip*: *Unrecognizable Answer Choices are Almost Always Wrong*

Answers with Latin phrases (such as *in loco parentis*) without an English translation or mere areas of the Constitution (such as Article 2, Section 1 Clause 5) that don't explain what they are (in other words, it should say "The Natural Born Clause") are generally wrong when there are more recognizable answers available. Don't be lured by the unknown. There's a reason you don't recognize it, and chances are, almost no one else taking the test that day recognizes it either.

This may surprise you, but it's common for bar exam takers to score higher on the actual bar exam than on any of their practice tests! Remember, most of the preparation course materials you're using are designed to prepare you for the worst. Although the questions on the bar exam will look a little different, sound a little less recognizable and throw you for a little bit of a loop, if you have prepared properly, you will have learned how to sort the potentially good from the clearly bad answers.

H. FAILING TO CREATE EXAM STRATEGIES AND TACTICS

There are some students who appear to prepare efficiently but fail to include prearranged strategies and tactics for each of the subject areas or question types on the exam. While some students are hardwired for creating such strategies and tactics, this important component of exam success needs serious attention.

1. Mistake #1: Not Having a Strategy For Responding to Multiple Choice Questions – Don't go to Las Vegas, go to Hawaii.

For multiple choice questions in general, strategies should be developed about what to read first, think first and so on. Once you start thinking in a way that sends you down the wrong road, it is too easy to get fouled up. Students often work through many multiple choice practice problems, but not with any significant strategies or tactics. Instead, the students just "do them" and then review the ones they answered incorrectly. They go to Las Vegas instead of Hawaii. *What?* Allow us to explain. When you go to Las Vegas, you go to gamble. That's exactly what you'll be doing if you don't have a real strategy on how to answer a bar exam question. You may end up thinking all too often, "The best answer feels like a 'C'!"

> The less you go to Las Vegas and gamble on answers, the better off you will be.

Instead, we want you to go to Hawaii. Hawaii is a beautiful place with clear water and fresh air. People usually leave Hawaii richer for the experience. We want you to feel confident and at ease when you take the bar exam, like someone swimming the Northshore of Hawaii – not like a panicked gambler on a losing streak at 2 a.m. in the main casino at Caesar's Palace. You'll feel more confident and relaxed if you have a strategy and an approach on how to answer these questions. In this book, we're going to offer you a set of Multistate "protocols" - meaning a way to approach questions from each of the 6 Multistate subjects. If you follow our approach and apply the rules correctly, you'll know exactly what to do and where to begin when you get to a difficult question – instead of rolling the dice and playing unreliable odds.

2. Mistake #2: Not Having a Strategy for Writing an Effective Essay

There are advance strategies that students ought to develop for essay answers, just like for multiple choice questions. Don't think that replicating the detailed and lengthy model answers to essays in your course materials is itself a writing strategy. (Can you really do that in the time allotted, anyway?). Have a writing structure down and know how to apply it on paper. Because the bar essays tend to have different objectives than law school questions and, significantly, often have detailed and multiple calls of the question rather than a simple "discuss," students without specific strategies often are at a disadvantage. They do not have an envisioned opening, a planned format, or a strategy for keeping on time. While students writing essays appear to be cool, calm and collected, often they are "machine gunning" information out in a random manner, hoping it will stick and score points. Once again, they're going to Vegas and playing the odds. That's not the most helpful approach to one of the most important tests in a law student's career.

I. TEST-TAKING JUDGMENT ERRORS

In addition to mistakes made during bar preparation, such as failing to develop strategies and tactics, students often make a lot of exam-time mistakes that impact their performance. These mistakes all can be arranged around a constellation of judgment errors. Let's walk through several of the larger errors.

1. Personal Maintenance

> Radical personal transformations
> before the bar exam generally
> don't help bar exam performance.

Personal maintenance is the "x" factor. This maintenance refers to how students take care of themselves for the "athletic contest" that is the bar exam. Maintenance involves sleeping, eating, and well-being activities such as exercising. For instance, some students continue "hard-core" studying the night before the exam and are tired the next day. Other students take a sleeping pill for the first time on the night prior to the exam, take up smoking, quit smoking or engage in other radical transformations of their personal habits right before the big test. The results can be disastrous. If they are not tired out for the exam, the students are disoriented or, at the least, out-of-sync. Other students change their diet and end up with stomach problems.

If you've been thinking about quitting a bad habit or adopting a new one, here's a tip: this is not the time! There's plenty of time for that later. For now, just stick to what you know and makes you feel comfortable.

There are some less worrisome problems that can still arise. If students have not thought out their lunch and dinner plans during the days of the exam, for example, they end up searching when they should be eating. Other students have poor lodging, based on travel distance to the exam site, distractions from a roommate, or the lodging itself (*e.g.,* the hotel is adjacent to train tracks, such as the one in the film, "My Cousin Vinnie," rumbling through at the same time each night).

2.   *Other Distractions*

Other distractions can be just as annoying. These include an unreliable watch, poor quality pens or pencils, or uncomfortable clothes. This last matter affects students who end up being too cold or too warm based on what they have worn to the exam, or too concerned about how they look instead of how they will take the exam. Trust us on this one - no one will be paying attention to you on exam day. Brad Pitt or Angelina Jolie could be sitting next to you and chances are, you're not going to even notice them. You're going to be too preoccupied.

3.   *Things to Watch Out For – Catching a Last Minute "Red-eye" to Las Vegas*

A lot of students might change their multiple choice answers incessantly or habitually cross out their responses on essays. They've already made it to Hawaii, but like a compulsive gambler, they feel the need to catch a quick red-eye flight back to Vegas and throw the dice. Chances are your first instinct is the right one, so don't go back and sink yourself into debt.

Another important fact is to make sure your flight information is accurate - in other words, make sure your multiple choice questions were answered sequentially and completely. You should be circling your answer choice in the Multistate exam booklet and then filling it in on the answer sheet. Can you imagine your horror if at question 187 you realize somewhere you skipped a question and the past 72 answers were filled in incorrectly? You're going to end up wasting 15 valuable minutes erasing and filling in blanks - if you even have that time left. This is absolutely crucial and we strongly advise you take this approach.

On essay exams, some students try to show off their intellect by offering unusual, and often insignificant, analysis, instead of discussing the obvious issues first. These students try to "out-think" the graders, rather than meet the objectives of the exam to ensure attorney competence.

There are other mistakes that students make, leading to bar exam failure, but these are the "top 10." The next section of the book examines the winning strategies and tactics that can assist students in passing the bar exam on the first try.

OK, **READY**? *Here we go.*

IV. QUALITIES OF SUCCESSFUL EXAM TAKERS

Chapter Points:
(1) Read, Think and Write Critically.
(2) Know Where You Are Going and What It Takes to Get You There.
(3) Commit to Learning the 'Big Rock' Issues.

A. INTRODUCING THE SUCCESSFUL BAR EXAMINEE

Remember that movie *The Matrix*? Wouldn't it be great if there was a magic red pill that you could take and suddenly find yourself in a world that allows you to do the impossible? Well, we've got some news for you. There isn't. Okay, relax. We don't mean to get you down. You're still going to find "how deep the rabbit hole really goes." Unfortunately, it's not going to be as easy as hooking you up to a supercomputer and feeding you thousands of bar rules. However, we can make it easier on you by telling you how to prepare for combat and that's exactly what this chapter is about.

In effect, the bar exam calls for a variety of attributes on your part. The primary attributes include the skills of reading, thinking and writing, the discipline to study effectively, the judgment to make sound and well-reasoned decisions and the poise to answer questions under time pressure. Our point is that these methods ARE your red pill. Don't take the blue pill. Keep reading and learn - and then you'll be as close as you can get to being Neo once you're in the complex 'Matrix' of the bar exam.

1. The Skills You Need Now

> The bar exam is a test of thinking,
> sandwiched between reading and writing.

"[A] good legal doctrine is like a good horse: you can ride it to the vicinity of the problem you need to solve, and then you must get down and walk."[1]

Unlike law school, where the typical essay issue spotter test revolves around "thinking like a lawyer," the bar examination contains multiple choice questions as well as essays and allegedly assesses attorney competence. Regardless of the differences in tests – and they are indeed significant – law school and bar exams alike require at least three different skills – critical reading, thinking, and writing – in a directed and probing fashion. You have to really concentrate and think carefully. As you can see, it isn't exactly like law school evaluation in retrospect.

Now, these three skills include a wide variety of tasks. For example, when answering multiple choice or essay questions remember that they all include the ability to translate facts into legal issues. In reading critically, you must distinguish important from unimportant facts and draw useful inferences from the important facts to frame the issue and begin legal analysis.

Critical thinking involves a family of mental aerobics. You'll use doctrinal protocols or frameworks (similar to assembling toys or machines, which often have displayed on the cover the phrase, "minor assembly required," while the instructions contain 847 simple steps). The frameworks, like blueprints, organize knowledge and provide roadmaps for more effective problem-solving. Your skill in this context means mastery of both frameworks and rules, not simply a little knowledge about a lot of different things.

Bar skills also require recall - how to remember and recapture the rules and principles – not mere "sky writing," the evanescent appearance and then disappearance of concrete knowledge. You're going to find that every time you learn a new

---

[1]   D. Robertson, *Eschewing Ersatz Percentages: A Simplified Vocabulary of Comparative Fault*, 45 St. Louis L. J. 831, fn 92 (2001) (quoting the author's recollection of a saying of his professor, Dean Leon Green).

bar rule, it's really easy to forget another one. You must hold on to your knowledge! Make sure you review material daily. Repetition is crucial. Keep yourself going without forgetting all the hard work you've already done!

In addition, thinking skills includes the strategic ability to answer multiple choice questions. These strategies employ the protocol of applying the "3i's" to a multiple choice question. The "3i's" – irrelevant, incomplete or incorrect – involve making a determination that answer choices are irrelevant, incomplete or incorrect. Remember, many of these answers will look similar or include a rule that looks like it could apply to the fact pattern, but up close and personal, you'll find that three of them are usually inferior answer choices.

To improve your skills, it's useful to practice with technique. A predicate technique is active, rather than passive, preparation. Active preparation involves a conscious and sustained effort to regularly do practice problems and write essays - even for non-essay subjects like Evidence, so you can master the rules in your head. After all, writing is just one expression of thinking. And fuzzy thinking often equals fuzzy writing. In particular, this technique involves simulation, applying study techniques to conditions that attempt to replicate the actual exam – especially time pressure. Creating a real simulation under time pressure is an important preparation strategy because it provides a "dress rehearsal" that synthesizes all of the other techniques. It'll make it much more comfortable on you when you actually enter the exam room.

Fuzzy writing is reflective of fuzzy thinking.

The use of smart study techniques is designed to help you score higher. After all, it's output that matters, not input. If you cram in a lot of studying, but none of it sticks, the output will be very weak indeed. To determine output levels, you've got to get feedback. Feedback is a learned skill, not something "hardwired" in most people. Real solid study techniques have a dual purpose – to improve the effectiveness of both preparation and for taking the actual exam.

> Your output, not input, is
> what counts.

Using exam strategies and tactics, both prior to and during the test, are essential to maximizing exam performance. Without strategies – effective strategies – it's like going to Vegas.

With such a large quantity of material on the examination, it's easy to lose sight of the fact that the skill of critical reading is a prerequisite to understanding and applying the rules. If you can't spot the important facts yielding the particular issue that will give you the answer – or read the call of the question accurately and with reasonable comprehension of what the question asks – no amount of brilliant legal analysis will save you from choosing a wrong answer. In a way, the bar examination should be viewed as a huge reading test under time pressure – can students read and translate issues into the language of the law and then respond to them correctly?

B. CRITICAL THINKING, READING AND WRITING

> The bar exam is really a huge
> reading test under time pressure.

1. *Critical Reading - The Whole Package*

Reading critically is an important skill for any law school examination and is particularly important for the bar examination. This skill is not discussed directly in bar review courses or in law school, but it's ironically the core of the Socratic method.

When a teacher calls on you, it's usually about a particular component of a case and the interpretive method to be used in figuring out what that part of the case means. You're usually expected to explain the legal significance of those words, particularly the facts or rationale used by the court. And so, you probably remember that when you read those cases, you wanted to be sure you actually understood what the rule from the case meant – otherwise, you were sitting in front of about 100 people unable to explain why "illusory promises" aren't considered valid consideration. If you had read carefully, you would remember that an illusory promise arises when there is something that looks like a promise to perform, but really isn't. If you weren't paying attention, well, we've just thrown you a bone.

Critical reading is a lot different than reading for pleasure. For starters, well . . . it's not a whole lot of fun. Don't expect to open those bar materials and find yourself riveted like you're pouring through a John Grisham or Tom Clancy novel. However, you will find yourself intrigued as you study - and the more you study, the more you'll find yourself curious to get the whole package.

Reading is an exercise in thinking.

Our point is that you have to be actively engaged in thinking – sorting, identifying and labeling – while reading. The critical reader draws inferences from the words, synthesizes and connects the inferences and evaluates the question and possible answers. Your job is to comprehend and remember the little nuances and distinctions because that's what's going to be tested on the bar exam. If you are reading critically, it's going to make the difference in understanding what a question is asking and being able to take the next step of actually selecting the right answer.

Reading critically is the gateway to legal reasoning and problem solving. The natural sequence for a test-taker is to read, then think, then act, although the succeeding action is really intertwined with thinking. The "primacy" of reading, however, is often overlooked. Reading is usually recognizing "trigger words" that allow the reader to spot the issues and analyze them. Identifying issues and judging which issues are the best ones to pursue is a critical skill.

How to read critically, however, is not something you may be "hardwired" to do - that is, naturally understand how to spot legal issues in a complex fact pattern. It may take work and lots of perspiration.

For example, the statement, "Jones slipped and fell on the sidewalk right where Adam had dropped his banana peel," has immediate implications in the law. Just like the statement, "Barbara was asked while testifying during cross-examination whether she had ever been convicted of grand theft auto." Both of these statements yield legal issues that can be discussed and analyzed by students. The first statement infers possible negligence and the second implies a possible impeachment method. The answers depend on the entire fact pattern, so you have to read carefully.

Lots of people, however, gloss over the salient words and just sort of throw them all together, like a big chocolate sundae. They just dig into that vanilla ice cream, scoop up some chocolate syrup and dig into some whipped cream, without pausing and evaluating the legal significance of each component.

Underlining everything, even in different colors,
is not critical reading.

What we're trying to get across is that people who just throw all those words together have problems. We call them *"en toto underliners."* They seemingly highlight or underline every single word in all paragraphs. Remember, if you highlight

47

everything, well, what's the difference if you hadn't highlighted it at all? This lack of discrimination undermines the critical nature of the reading enterprise. The same is true for the converse approach – those students who do not circle at all, underline or make notes about key words, phrases or paragraphs are also confusing themselves. These students attempt to spot the legal significance of words and keep only a mental file on them. That's not a good move.

> Some words in bar exam fact patterns count more than others.

On a test, especially the bar examination, facts come first, unlike in the classroom, where cases are discussed before you're handed a plate full of test questions. On the Multistate bar exam, facts are provided first in the form of very compact hypotheticals. This throws off a lot of people who aren't used to the format.

In addition, critical reading requires students to locate what course and area of law the question concerns. The call of the question won't always indicate what area of the law or what issue the question calls you to answer. Many law school exams simply have a call of the question that includes the word "discuss." On the bar exam, the call of the question doesn't usually state the legal basis for the question, and in fact, many of the answer choices are simply facts presented to the student that relate to a rule of law. What are we getting at? You've got to translate these facts into the pertinent course, legal rule and its elements.

When analyzing multiple choice questions, translate the words into one of three categories:

(a) *Background Words:* Much of the question involves background words, providing context, nuance and a story to the problem at hand.

(b) ***Words of Exam-Taking Significance:*** These are words
that dictate the parameters and orientation of a question,
including asking for the best or worst argument or role-
play.

(c) ***Words of Legal Significance:*** These are words in the
facts patterns or responses that trigger legal issues.

Some words have legal significance. By this, we mean
that they relate to legal rules, defenses, and causes of action.
Examples are "objection," which relates to trial and evidence
law, and "defendants," which also relates to trials, evidence, and
other subject areas. The word "agreement" has great
significance in contract law. The words "Congress passed a law"
has great significance in constitutional law. The words of
potential legal significance should be connected to the particular
rule, element, defense, or cause of action by the good test-taker.
The skill of translation is really a large part of critical reading.
When a good reader reads a word of legal significance, the
reader will make that notation in her mind. A poor reader, on the
other hand, will simply skim over the words, not grasping the
entire significance of them.

The same skill is required for "interpreting" the
significance of test-taking words. In most responses, a
conclusion is given first, such as "A will win," and then an
important test-taking word will follow, such as "because" or "if."
These words – "because," "if," "unless" – are critical to
unraveling the focus and propriety of each answer choice. Thus,
if an answer choice reads something to the effect of "A will win,
unless the contract provides for a condition subsequent," the
word "unless" has critical significance in understanding the
truthfulness and accuracy of the response. The word "unless"
completely changes the answer choice so that instead of saying,
"A will win," it means "B will win if...." Good test-takers look
for these words and immediately understand the role they play in
the question. Poor test-takers skim over these words and look at
the answer choices with the belief that all words are equal,

failing to categorize and highlight the particular words in question.

Whether it's an essay or multiple choice test question, reading critically is a predicate skill. Without critical reading, you may overlook the issue in the problem and lose points despite having complete and accurate knowledge of the subject matter. Critical reading entails being able to associate legal principles and rules to the facts embedded in the hypotheticals. It further involves prioritizing the legal implications derived from the facts – which of the potential legal issues is the most important? What's the hierarchy of legal issues? The connection between the person's knowledge of the subject matter and the issue itself is reading critically.

2. Critical Thinking - A Learning Pyramid of Skills

LEARNING PYRAMID

(Lowest) Knowledge:
Knowledge of
the legal words.
(Higher) Understanding: Knowing each and
every element.
(Higher Still) Issue-Spotting: Determining which
area of law applies.
(Even Higher) Problem-Solving: Applying facts
to the law.
(Highest) Judgment: Choosing the better forks in the road.

This learning pyramid – called a taxonomy by the pros – is based on one offered way back in 1956 by Dr. Benjamin Bloom, published as A Taxonomy of Education Objectives.

Critical thinking is really a family of skills that range from a lower order to a higher order of cognitive analysis. Thinking for bar exam purposes is not a passive, internal activity, but one that is connected to different types of performances. Thinking critically can be broken down into the component parts of the pyramid shown above.

Knowledge

The lowest level or type of learning is knowledge, a simple knowledge of the legal words that are used to formulate the rules and principles of law. The knowledge of the rules and principles is not a general, hazy version of the law, but rather a specific, precise and accurate statement of the elements of the cause of action or the defenses. This is one of the areas in which law students get confused. They believe that a general, overall understanding of the subject matter, without being able to provide the details, is sufficient. Unfortunately, they are sorely mistaken and often end up failing the exam as a result.

Understanding

Immediately after knowledge is *understanding* – an ability to explain and use specific definitions. You need to be able to explain *each and every element* of the definition. For example, if negligence requires duty, breach, causation, and damages, you should be able to explain what each of these four elements means. Describing a duty as "requiring a duty" is inadequate and circular. You've got to be able to understand what it means to create an obligation of care to those within a zone of danger.

Issue-Spotting

> Issue-spotting is like being asked to find the chicken aisle in the supermarket when all of the aisle signs have been removed.

The next level of learning is *issue-spotting*. This is the heart of thinking that relates to critical reading. You need to be able to determine which area of law applies to particular facts and why that area of law is better pursued than alternative possibilities. This order of learning is particularly important on the bar examination where all labels have been taken off the questions so that students have no idea in which course the question lies, let alone the particular area within that course.

Problem-Solving

After issue-spotting, students have to learn how to problem solve – the mainstay of law school courses and examinations. Unfortunately, to reach problem-solving, you've got to first show some competency with the three lower levels of learning – knowledge, understanding, and issue-spotting. In problem-solving, you learn to use the facts and apply the law to those facts through *legal analysis*. It is here where you need to understand how each element is proven based on particular facts provided in the problem.

Judgment

> Judgment is what you use when choosing between two seemingly correct responses on Multistate bar examination questions.

The final or highest level of learning is *evaluation or judgment*, which involves your assessment of what arguments are better and why, including the relative strength of arguments and their likelihood of success. It is the highest level of critical thinking and important on bar examinations (and least taught in law school). Judgment is what you use when choosing between two answer choices on a Multistate bar examination problem or which defense to raise first in an essay question.

There is another way to look at how to categorize critical thinking. The lowest common denominator is the rules of the cases, statutes or Constitution - the elements of rules of law, claims, or defenses. These elements should be memorized with precision and accuracy so you'll understand them and be able to recite and communicate them to a study partner or in an essay later on. To do this, you've got to make sure you know what the elements mean. Further, you should be able to provide illustrations and make up some of your own hypotheticals. A great way to test yourself on this ability is by practicing with study partners. If your partner wants you to explain something, explain the rule, the elements and then create your own hypothetical. Last, but not least, since the bar examiners love exceptions, know the exceptions to the rules as well as the rules themselves.

How to Get to Understanding

To best "know" the rules and understand them, there are at least three steps to take while studying: (1) learn the elements of the cause of action or defense; (2) explain the meaning of the cause of action or defense; (3) prepare examples of the cause of action or defense.

Many students "learn" the rules and principles of different areas of the law but do not do so completely and precisely. And that's the key! You need to know the entire rule and its exceptions because it's those nuances on which the examiners will test. If you master them, you will be the master of the bar exam – rather than it being a master of you.

> *Know the elements of rules and what they mean (using only key words or phrases). For the bar exam, it is all about understanding, not simply rote memorization.*

For example, some students can describe the rules generally, but cannot boil them down to their component, bedrock pieces, namely their elements. Thus, for negligence, you probably know that duty, breach, actual and proximate causation and damages are required. For burglary, the elemental description is the breaking and entering at nighttime of the dwelling house of another with the intent to commit a felony therein. You've got to know those elements like the back of your hand.

3. Critical Writing

Okay, if you really want to 'score' on the essay portion of the state bar exam, you've got to be able to write critically. Writing critically is very different than other types of legal writing, even writing for a traditional law school exam. You need to know that organization and structure are very important, as is spotting the issues presented – rather than simply including the information "somewhere" or "generally" in the responses. Critical writing implies a conscious decision to create paragraphs with a single point, from issues, rules, analysis and conclusions, to a conscious expression of analysis. For students who write reflexively and with habits taken from different writing contexts and learning experiences, critical writing is a skill that promotes the clear communication of ideas and knowledge.

Now, let's give you an example of how to begin a bar exam essay. Here's how you might start any typical contracts essay:

a. The Question Asked

[Usually, when you are asked a question in contracts, there is often a lawsuit brewing or pending between two of the parties, say A and B.] While starting with a conclusion is fine and sometimes preferable, always keep in mind what the question asked of you. You want to answer the examiners' questions – not one of your own. So practice writing their questions, using the parties and the general legal basis for the dispute, if one exists. Then and only then, start with the basic steps of an answer for that course. So, for example, the first two steps in a contract answer could be laid out generally as follows:

> *b.   What Contract Law Applies?*

What law governs a contract issue? The applicable law is generally the U.C.C. (Uniform Commercial Code) or common law. The U.C.C. applies to the sale of goods.

> Here, the proper law to apply is _____ because...

> *c.   Was a Contract Formed?*

For a contract to exist, there must be an offer, an acceptance of the offer, and consideration. An offer is a request to enter into an agreement. An acceptance is an assent to the offer and consideration is something of value or forbearance.

> Here, there was an offer because _____.

Some contracts questions involve typical subcomponents and must be set up with scaffolding (subcomponents) instead of just dumping an answer and some rationalizations for that answer.

C. COMMITMENT TO PASSING THE BAR EXAM

> A successful bar exam test-taker is committed to passing the exam.

1. Get Disciplined!

Remember the Karate Kid? Remember how his teacher had him paint his fence a particular kind of way? "Wax on, wax off!" the teacher would say repetitively. The Karate Kid thought it was nonsense, but in the end he realized that every one of those painting strokes was a special kind of defensive karate move. Okay, we're the teacher and you've got to get out that paintbrush! We're going to get you disciplined and show you some pretty cool brush strokes along the way.

Discipline is what you bring to the table with respect to the nature and focus of preparation. Without the discipline to follow through on good intentions, the intentions will wither away. You know they say the road to ruin was paved with good intentions; well, they were talking about the bar exam.

Disciplined bar exam-takers possess a resolute commitment to passing the test. A commitment shows up as a set of practices indicating that the test is a top priority and not merely viewed as another annoying task blending in with the nonsense of everyday life. Commitment level is a good barometer of a person's intensity and studying levels, but it's never a guarantee. Being disciplined is simply better than the alternative.

Responsibility also encompasses self-management, which includes time management, habit management and mental preparation. In addition, you've got to know when you study best, under what conditions, how long, and having the discipline to maintain a pre-designed schedule – or to modify it intelligently.

Discipline and commitment are what you do, not what you think.

2. How Badly Do You Want It . . . Really?

While the overwhelming number of people who study for the bar exam seem to want to become lawyers, they don't really demonstrate through their conduct a desire to pass the $&*% Exam. The commitment tends to wander during the monotonous and often lengthy period of preparation, especially when no one else is looking. At times you may feel very, very lethargic over the whole process. The best way to avoid this is to stay on it. You've got to get in the zone. The more you do, the more you'll want to do. The more you avoid it, the harder it will be to get back on the horse. It will seem like a real pain.

3. Treat the Exam as a "Big Rock"

> The "Big Rocks" are our
> priorities in life.

A "big rock" is a significant part of a person's life that demands direct attention. It's a top priority. While many students want to pass the exam, they prioritize other things above it. Many test-takers are working, have family obligations, friends, and other responsibilities. And there is no-one looking over their shoulders saying "Don't do that." While it is not recommended that students simply drop their worldly responsibilities – especially regarding family and income – it is important to shuffle obligations to shift the emphasis prior to the bar exam to preparing for the examination.

4. Illustration: Well-Rounded Ted

Ted was a "well-rounded" person in law school, meaning that he was involved in moot court competitions, the Environmental Law Club, and the International Law Journal, as well as participating in the American Bar Association as a student representative. Ted studied moderately hard, attended classes, and clerked for a law firm as well. When it came time to prepare for the bar examination, Ted replicated his law school experience, doing volunteer work, becoming involved in a tennis league, and studying with a whole group of students with diverse interests. While Ted found himself tired at the end of each day, it was not really from bar exam preparation but from the multiplicity of activities he had created for himself. After the bar exam, Ted felt just like he did with some of his law school

57

exams, that he did enough. Except he had not. Ted was surprised to learn that he had flunked by three points. When Ted dropped the multitasking lifestyle and devoted himself full-time to bar preparation, with one or two other activities primarily used to vent and let off steam, he passed the test with flying colors.

5.   *Every Day Counts*

"The only real currency is time." – Isaac Asimov

Okay, some people love the challenge of feeling their backs pressed firmly to the wall, having to cram for an exam and producing at the last possible second. Even if this does not describe you, one of the bar exam's dirty tricks is that it makes it difficult to realize that the first few weeks of bar preparation, even the very first day, are as important as the last few weeks or last day, and that consistency and regular effort matter. It's because you're dividing your studying time. The first day may be about a property rule and some criminal law, rules and law that may be featured prominently on the exam. Look, that first day isn't any less important than it was in a law school class. That first day is the beginning, middle and end of those rules you are studying. You either get it that week or say goodbye! You're not going to have too much time to come back to it later because later, you'll be studying another set of rules. Got it?

Acting as if studying matters three months before the exam as much as it does the week before the test is difficult to do. In fact, the easy monotony of the studying lulls one into the opposite belief that it doesn't "really count" until the test is almost there. Wrong!

6. *Here is the Real Question: How Much Does It Cost to Fail?*

It is not simply a desire to pass that often motivates, but an urgency to avoid failure. You need to realize that failing the bar has a lot of costs, and a new sign in the bathroom should read, "How Much Would It Cost Me To Flunk?" There are a ton of costs, ranging from financial – there is a delay in practicing law and many employers will reduce salaries of people on a clerk status as compared to an attorney status – to emotional costs. For some people, the shame attached to failing the bar only kicks in after it occurs, and they realize that they must sit for the test again. In addition, there are other financial costs as well, including the cost of loans, which kick in six months after graduation from law school on many occasions. Look, don't let the shame factor get you down. That's a bunch of nonsense. But spending thousands of dollars, delaying your career and your life, well, that's no fun. Take it from us. We've heard lots of stories from people who have been through it and not one of them ever said they were glad they got to do it all over again. If you're already re-taking it, you know what we mean.

Steve says:

*Every person I've tutored over the past decade or so has sung a common song: failing the bar is a big blow. It is not just the financial costs but also the self-esteem and status issues that materialize. Despite the exam **not** being an intelligence test, failing it creates a lot of difficulties. Don't go down that road.*

7. Illustration: "Time is A Jar of Marbles"

Imagine having a jar of marbles, filled to the brim. There's way too many to count off hand, but there is a limited number in the jar, nonetheless. When a marble is removed from the jar, it can never be replaced. Every day, another marble must be removed from the jar. What was once a multicolored work of art is slowly crumbling into simply another empty jar.

Now imagine that each marble represents a block of studying time, such as six hours. Every day, another marble

59

must be removed from the jar. Eventually, there won't be any left at all. These "withdrawals" cannot be replaced by deposits in any way.

We can act like the marbles are endless and pretend the last few matter more. But if we spend the time to look at them, we can see that they are unique and irreplaceable. Each marble can represent progress and hard work or simply roll away unused. That's our choice - but we cannot affect the marbles disappearing.

This is not to say every hour must be spent studying - far from it. Do what you have to do. Also, remember to take regular breaks and go for walks and watch a movie without pretending to be studying. Don't fool yourself. If you want to watch TV for a while, just watch it. If you try to do both, what happens is that you won't focus on your questions, you'll pick a stupid answer and just depress yourself. We speak from personal experience.

8. Remove Temptations

If you want it badly enough, you have to make it easy to study. People on diets should not go out and buy chocolate, ice cream, cookies and cake to keep lying around the kitchen. People committed to passing the bar exam should have a dedicated place to study with as few interruptions and distractions as possible. Don't tempt yourself.

9. Dedicate a Study Place

We talked before about location. People thrive in different kinds of environments – from small towns to big cities, from the cold to the hot and so on. The same goes for studying. There are people who want every pencil to be parallel with each other and those who know exactly where everything is in what otherwise appears to be a total mess. Regardless of the environment created, it should be dedicated (at least in large part) with the objective of studying in mind – not a place for play or relaxation. While no ribbon-cutting ceremony is necessary, the choice is ribbon-cutting important. From the mundane (good lighting?) to the esoteric (is it ergonomic?), there are important questions to consider and confront. If passing the bar exam is that important, where and how a person prepares should be "front burner" issues. Just make yourself comfortable. Be yourself.

10. Go Ahead and Do It!

Distractions come in many different sizes and shapes. In addition to the media – television, films, newspapers, magazines, etc. – you're probably bombarded daily with alternatives to studying. To minimize distractions, you've got to prioritize study time, generally placing bar preparation first. Just wake up and DO IT. Go to your study place and get in gear! Don't waste time dreading it. Once you start and get the wheels turning, trust us on this - you won't even remember you're there. Worrying about studying is a LOT worse than actually studying. Remember that.

11. Display the "Do Not Disturb" Sign

> Put daily distractions like e-mail
> on a lower priority level.

Clearing time is not as easy as it sounds. In today's busy world where cell phones and beepers and advancing technology allow people to stay "connected" 24 hours a day, it is difficult to find uninterrupted time in which to study. For many people, attending the bar review course becomes instantly cleared time, but that is often insufficient.

The goal, therefore, is to identify time usage each day and look for spaces in which bar prep can occur. If a person has no responsibilities other than studying for the bar exam, there ought to be little trouble identifying preparation time. If, however, conflicts exist, this labeling will be more difficult.

If uninterrupted prep time is not available, consider sharing time with other tasks. One obvious location is in the car, where driving often is one of several activities. Drivers listen to the radio, talk on a cell phone, dictate, gaze at the scenery, talk with passengers and eat and drink. "Car time" can be used for bar preparation as much as any other time of the day, although it is not as valued as "study-room" time, which can be singularly devoted to bar preparation. (There's no need to watch out for other drivers in your study room.) Mealtime is another place to "steal" some bar prep time, if needed. This type of "time share" should occur only based on need – if possible, driving time should be spent focused on the road exclusively and mealtime on eating.

> *We recommend that you study in the car by talking out loud – but to still keep your eyes on the road.*

12. Treat Bar Prep as Your First Law Job

Another way to evidence a steadfast commitment to passing the bar is to treat it like your first job – which, in a way, it is. Like most jobs, studying involves some interesting and not so interesting activities; it is repetitive and usually occurs on a regularly scheduled basis.

An employee is expected to show up at work on time and stay the entire day. (If this information is surprising to you, then this book will be really useful.) The employee is expected to work and work hard whether she feels like it or not. The employee is expected to produce results. There is no reason to treat preparations for the bar exam in a different manner. In fact, top attorneys often say preparation is the key to lawyering – and it's a key to the bar exam as well.

Just because bar prep is treated like work does not mean it has to be absolutely horrible. Students should include variety and try to make it as interesting as possible.

Studying for the bar exam really is your first job; treat it that way.

13. *Exercising Judgment*

"No matter how far you walk down the wrong road, turn back." – Old proverb

Judgment means the ability to make effective decisions about preparation and the exam itself. Discipline indicates the ability to self-manage time, habits, and mental preparedness. Your skill means the ability to perform all of the tasks the exam demands. Finally, poise means successfully negotiating the often subtle, but nefarious, effects of time pressure during the actual exam.

Your exercise in judgment relates to decisions all along the bar preparation continuum, from which prep course to take, if any, to exam-time decisions of how much to write in response to an essay question. Exercising judgment also involves the existence and nature of self-assessment, particularly the effectiveness of the preparations. In this regard, judgment concerns the relationship between the inputs and outputs of studying. In other words, judgment involves the connection between what you put in and what you get out of it.

A significant component of judgment is understanding exactly what is required to successfully prepare for the bar exam. It extends to an understanding of the subject matter emphasized on the exam, how it is tested, and the skills needed to pass the examination – from reading, to knowledge, to writing. The more you are conscious about the skills required, the better the opportunity to practice and sharpen your skills.

Judgment is inherently intertwined with mental prep-aration. *The psychology of bar preparation is perhaps as important as the actual learning process*, since it is a crucial corollary to the performance component. Even with a resolute commitment, the allocation of sufficient time, self-management, the acquisition of preparation and exam-taking techniques, and the use of simulation, all might be for naught if the test-taker ignores the mental component. This component prevents those studying for the bar exam from becoming overwhelmed, exceedingly nervous or excessively distracted from the task at hand.

14. Managing Time Effectively

"If it jams, force it. If it breaks, it needed replacing anyway." – Murphy's Laws on Life

Time management sounds difficult and it is, especially in a bar examination setting. Time management means many things, from finding the time to study, to finding uninterrupted time, to finding time in the most productive part of the day, whatever part that may be for the student in question. Time management problems are legendary.

Common Time Management Mistakes

a. Saving a Subject or the State Law Part of the Exam for Last

In some bar review courses, the state law portion of the course follows that of the multistate law. One inference is that state law is secondary to the six multistate areas and, in any event, ought to be studied last. As a consequence of this kind of thinking, students often under-perform on the state law portion of the exam – which often is weighted equally to the Multistate day. Instead, you should study the state law subjects simultaneously with the Multistate topics – *e.g.,* Multistate criminal law and state criminal law – and treat the state law as a "big rock," too, regardless of where it is located in the bar review course.

> b. *Skipping Subjects Entirely – Due to Time Mismanagement or the Misplaced Assumption it Won't Be Tested*

You may leave out a doctrinal topic or even an entire course given the subjective (and often unreasonable) belief that it will not be tested, either on the Multistate exam or the state test. Instead, do at least one rule a week in each course (or almost every course), diminishing coverage pressures. The week's rule should be placed on the schedule and carried over if additional work is needed.

> c. *Skipping Rules or Doctrines Because of Their Complexity or Difficulty*

Don't skip rules like the Best Evidence Rule just because they are difficult.

It is only natural to avoid rules, doctrines or subjects that appear to range from inscrutable to impossible. If it is a highly tested topic, that is definitely not a good idea. If you're adverse to Property or Constitutional Law, for example, you have to make special efforts to schedule rules training in those courses. The same goes for particular doctrines or topics.

15. *A Failure to Prioritize: Thinking All Topics Are Created Equal*

Don't kill yourself trying to learn EVERYTHING. Instead, learn what you NEED to KNOW to pass. To get the most out of studying, learning the most important topics first not only is common sense, but helps psychologically as well.

(Remember, it's not necessary to score an "A" or get recognized as achieving one of the highest scores.)

There are some topics in each course that are more heavily tested than others. The consequence of these disparities is that some subjects ought to be placed on a priority study list – they are the "big rocks" of the exam, unlike the "little pebbles" that remain.

16. Illustration: The Big Rocks

A geology class on a field trip to a beach area was challenged by the professor to fill up their buckets with as much rocks and dirt as they could. One student put in lots of sand and dirt and was unable to get the big rocks in the bucket. The next student poured in a little sand and some rocks and a little more sand and some rocks and was still unable to get all the big rocks in the bucket. The last student filled up the bucket with all the big rocks first and then filled in all the cracks with sand and smaller rocks. The meaning of the story is that it is important to prioritize and study the big "rocks" first.

The big rocks matter the most. Fit the little pebbles in around them, not vice versa.

17. Big Rocks for the Multistate Bar Exam – What you Really Need to Know

a. Evidence

Hearsay is one of the big rocks. It is a large part of the evidence content on the bar exam. Within hearsay, knowing what is not offered for the truth of the matter asserted and what is not hearsay under the Federal Rules of Evidence by statute (admissions and special prior statements of a witness) are important. Things like the best evidence rule, however, are better known as the wrong answer on the bar exam. (Not always, just often enough!) While it is often a distractor and sometimes a correct answer, that is much less important than understanding the hearsay rule or mastering impeachment and character evidence.

b. Torts

As noted earlier, negligence is the big rock in this area. While strict liability and intentional torts are useful, you should know negligence backwards and forwards. This includes negligence shortcuts, such as negligence per se and *res ipsa loquitur*, and standards of care (e.g. in a medical malpractice case).

c. Contracts

The big rock here is contract formation, and the big caveat is whether the U.C.C. or common law applies. Make that distinction right away, based on whether the problem involves a sale of goods. You should know everything about contract formation, including the nuances of unilateral contracts, offers, firm offers and advertisements, and not worry *as much* about third-party beneficiaries and assignments (although they are still important).

d. Criminal Law

Substantive criminal law most often tests the mental state required for crimes as well as defenses. It also widely tests the Fourth and Fifth Amendment in criminal procedure questions. Learn those search warrant exceptions and definitely learn which confession scenarios will be admissible and which won't.

e. Property

There are many rocks for property and often no single big rock. In recent times, the bar examiners seem to embrace testing mortgages, so really study those mortgages, since they seem to be more important every test administration. Traditional first year subjects, like future interests, encumbrances, and adverse possession, count as well. Recording statutes also pop up a lot.

f. Constitutional Law

You should know powers and limits equally but want to focus on the First Amendment, Equal Protection, Due Process, and other such limits in some detail. Excavating the First Amendment, in particular, will yield lots of distinctive pieces, from the freedom of speech, to the free exercise of religion, to the Establishment Clause. Also learn the hierarchy of powers so you know how to deal with express or implied conflicts between federal and state law.

Those are just some of the big "rocks" on which students should focus and spend more time really learning than other subjects.

18. Poise

> *Metabolize time pressure – that's poise.*

Poise refers to the test-taker's ability to metabolize time pressure so it has a minimal adverse impact on exam performance. Yes, metabolize sounds like digestion. Without poise, advances in the other three traits may be for naught. The effect of time pressure often is underestimated, distorting performance in many ways. Even if a person has the knowledge, skill, judgment and discipline to succeed, time pressure can warp and destroy it all. That is why simulation of exam questions is such an important component of bar preparation. Simulated practice doesn't make perfect – but it sure helps with poise.

V. GOALS ARE EVERYTHING - A SCHEDULE FOR BAR EXAM SUCCESS

Chapter Points:
(1) Study Schedule.
(2) Get Your Timing Down.

Some Important Points:
(1) Spontaneous studying usually fizzles out.
(2) Having daily detailed goals helps.
(3) Scheduling is a skill.

A. GOALS

While "winging it" can be a successful approach to the bar exam, most bar-takers (and attorneys) try to fully prepare. Why do even the best lawyers prepare for the bar exam when they go to another jurisdiction? Because having a plan is essential. The first step in effective preparation is detailing when, what, where and how learning will take place. Writing that plan down in the form of a schedule, rather than just thinking or talking about it, makes a difference.

One of the most important parts in creating a bar exam study plan is having identifiable goals. Many students think that studying for the bar is just about input, what they learn while sitting and listening and reading and that all that input turns into output for the exam. But it's not that simple. You've got to be able to verbalize and write the rules and elements as you learn them and explain what they mean. Despite what you may believe, rote memorization isn't going to cut it. Your bar review classes are very important, but those are just the raw ingredients. You need to organize them and then use them to create "output." You need to be able to understand and explain to your peers what the rules and elements mean and especially how to apply them.

70

Output

So the goal is output - what knowledge you really understand and take with you. If you can't recall it quickly and accurately, it doesn't count. On the bar exam, note "dumps" - of outlines memorized verbatim - generally don't count either. So how do you acquire this output?

A good test is whether you understand and can state a rule and its meaning out loud in 30 seconds or less. Can you communicate the rules to others in a clear and very concise way? Can you write it out? Here's another test regarding whether you've moved your "input" into the output box. Use multiple choice questions to write essays. That's right, actually write out your analysis to a few multiple choice questions - what the issue is, why the wrong answers are wrong and why the right one is right. Remember, your goal is to understand and ultimately master the frameworks of the six multistate subjects and numerous state law subjects. It's just as important to know why the wrong answers are wrong as why the right answers are right. People who skim schedule input NOT output - and that's missing the point. Studying one subject per day is actually counter-productive because you're missing one of the most important parts of funneling for the bar - which is making sure your input becomes output.

B. TIMING?

1. When

Give the test the time it needs, if not the time it deserves.

Employment

If money is not an issue, it is often best to devote undivided attention to bar exam preparation and not work. There are some people, however, who like working because it is a

71

welcome distraction. Others simply need to work for financial reasons. Just make sure you give it a little more time than needed rather than less – the extra week or two or three of bar studying could save months of aggravation and stress down the road.

How Many Months

There is no magic number as to how many months it takes to prepare for the bar exam. A rolling start that increases in strength and duration works for some. Others need a discrete amount of time that allows for their undivided attention. A general rule is that 2 to 3 months of *full-time study* is a standard minimum. If significant deficiencies in skills exist, more than the traditional two plus months separating the end of the semester and the bar exam may be warranted.

How Many Hours a Day

One yardstick is to treat the bar preparations as a full-time job and to allocate studying time accordingly. It is generally not a good idea to try to study every waking hour and engage in "overkill" right from the start – bar exam burnout is a serious potential problem.

Studying for the bar exam is your first job in the law – treat it that way.

---

2. *What*

While knowing what to study appears obvious, our experience has been that some students make a hazardous wrong turn when making this decision. A lot of people think they should study entire courses equally, when some aspects of each course are tested more frequently. On the other hand, some people think they don't have to practice writing essays for the bar exam because they "practiced" during the last set of law school examinations a month before. Other students believe their scores on certain subjects will carry them over their low scores on other subjects, which typically isn't the case.

> *In approaching the bar exam, it is important to understand a basic rule – to succeed, you've got to keep both the "big picture" in mind AND pay attention to the details.*

Many test-takers lose sight of the "big picture" or the details along the way. The "big picture" means the overall *frameworks* for each of the substantive courses (the blueprints) and test-taking techniques and structures for answering multiple choice questions and writing essays. "Global" learners like the big picture. The "details," on the other hand, are the *elements* of the rules and, more importantly, the *explanations*, *examples*, and *exceptions* to those rules as well. Those who like the details are the sequential learners.

For example, it is helpful to know that globally the Privileges and Immunities Clause of Article IV Section 2 is a limit on *state* discrimination against non-residents, but it is just as useful to know that sequentially, the Clause does not apply to discrimination against non-residents for recreation. It's also important to be able to distinguish the Article IV Privileges and Immunities Clause from the one in the 14th Amendment. Knowing the details precisely – and being able to recall the knowledge quickly – is extremely important.

Students should make a solid decision about what to study and when. Without such overt, known decision-making, all of the students' efforts may go for naught. They might work extremely hard – but not in an effective way. People describe this problem as "spinning their wheels." NASCAR and bar prep may have more in common than people believe.

3. *Where*

The answer is not always in the library.

As noted earlier, it is not always a "no-brainer" as to where someone should study for the bar. Because significant amounts of time are needed in an environment that avoids numerous distractions – like the beach – the studying location may differ from that of law school. As a general rule, avoid "polluted environments" – places filled with distractions. It may not be a distraction to study in a place with a high noise or energy level, but that ought to be a conscious choice.

Look beyond the surface. What may seem to be the quietest place at first glance may be far from conducive for studying. Libraries may be noisy and very social, while the privacy of one's home may have nearby refrigerators and several remote controls available for easy television access. On the other hand, a coffee shop or bookstore may be very quiet during certain hours and excellent places in which to focus. Big bookstores, like Barnes & Noble and Borders, also can be quiet enough places where you can work, and they also have other people working and studying so you feel inclined to study as well and not just get lost in the tranquility and isolation of your apartment or house. Big bookstores are also conducive to both individual and group studying or discussions. They also usually have some pretty good coffee and cookies at the café, so keep that in mind. You deserve an occasional perk, right?

Those people who like studying to music or in a certain manner – *e.g.*, standing up – shouldn't abandon those methods completely – but you should really try to focus on practicing questions in the same manner you'll be taking the test - sitting down and plowing away. Remember, they're not going to let you take your iPod into the exam and listen to Jim Morrison and the Doors sing "Light My Fire" while you hammer away at Constitutional Law. Also, it helps to have alternatives - when a particular locale gets "stale," it may be useful to turn elsewhere.

The studying environment does matter and should be taken seriously.

4. *How*

---

*The real question is how to study **effectively**.*

Knowing how to study is perhaps the most difficult question of all. The question is not simply about studying but how to study *effectively* – how to maximize efficiency in the time allotted. The answer depends – of course – on how the particular person learns best, considering such factors as how the person studies best and under what circumstances.

Having a good schedule is a large part of time management and it is more than that – it is the "quality control" system, the feedback device, the backup beeper that lets the driver know he or she is getting too close to something behind the vehicle. While many students surrender their control over scheduling to the bar review courses, they end up not having a history of maintaining a detailed schedule. It's not a bad idea to use the bar class schedule, but remember this – if you're not getting Property, it doesn't do much good to hop over to Criminal Law. Keep a schedule – but use your common sense. You can plan your schedule around the commercial bar review courses, but those are geared toward the masses and, by necessity, are not customized for the individual. Here are some important scheduling points.

a. *Schedule Output, Not Input*

Output is what matters, meaning, what you take with you to use on the exam.

For a lot of people, scheduling involves only "inputting," that is, how the student will spend time. Instead, scheduling ought to be done on a much broader plane. It really includes at a minimum four separate categories – goals, input (or activities), follow-up, and feedback on performance or accomplishments. "Output" means what you have learned – really learned and understood – so that you can teach that rule or subject to others on demand. To demonstrate output, you have to be able to say it or write it.

b. Studying Blocks

Don't simply schedule the entire day; schedule workable blocks such as one hour increments. Also include breaks. Be realistic. People need to stretch their legs and walk around – even during marathon study programs. A fairly recent study showed that taking a walk also promotes brain activity, so sitting in your seat without moving for hours is bad for the circulation and your studying.

c. McNuggets

> *Study not by course but by rules or doctrinal areas – course walls no longer exist for the bar.*

Studying "McNuggets" means to schedule one rule or doctrine at a time – not an entire course or even subject area. The goal is to obtain mastery of the topic before moving on to the next topic or subject. Thus, those students who sit down to review "Torts" often learn a little bit about a lot, something that is not very helpful in answering the precise and nuanced questions on the bar exam. Make a decision to learn the difference for instance between intervening and superseding causes. Learn the differences between *res ipsa* and negligence per se. Understand how products liability can be situated in both strict liability and negligence. (Comparisons are part of deep understanding, so make them a part of your studying.) Taking a solid 30 minutes to understand a concept, and perhaps work on a couple of multiple choice questions or writing sample essay paragraphs on them, is more valuable than spending several hours on Torts and walking away with a jumble of different areas of law.

> Study McNuggets – One rule or
> doctrine at a time.

d. *Variety*

Those students who study only one subject at a time often find the singularity mind-numbingly boring. In addition, the bar exam jumbles subjects together, making variety reflect the test more accurately. Thus, studying one subject at a time is not reflective of the test and is likely disadvantageous. It is helpful to mix in at least two subjects a day, just like a meal, where it is useful to have side dishes, appetizers, and an entrée, not just an extra-large entree.

e. *Test Yourself*

> *If it is understanding that counts,*
> *how do you know if you understand?*

In preparing for the exam, you're probably going to find yourself engaging in a mixture of reading, listening to lectures, writing essays and doing multiple choice problems. But how do you know if what you are doing is effective? How do you know if all that effort is working? The answer is getting feedback on your methods - from yourself. The follow-up is just as important as the initial task. If reading is done, try recalling what was learned out loud. If you finished a series of problems, don't just review questions for whether they were answered correctly, but whether you did the proper analysis and, more importantly, whether you can articulate (out loud) why the incorrect responses in each question are wrong. It sounds unnecessary, right? Well, if you don't know WHY you got something right and why the wrong answers were wrong, you could just be getting lucky. And what did we say about Lady Luck on the bar exam? Not the nicest person, so let's keep her out of the picture and rely solely on ourselves, shall we?

f. Feedback

> *Feedback matters; give some to yourself regularly.*

Feedback means you should try to construct benchmarks in studying to get an idea of where you stand. Don't use time as a way to measure your progress. Don't use how many questions you've done either. Come on, you know the drill – you could be sitting at a table for hours on end and you may have answered 1000 questions, but so what?! What can you recite? What rules and elements do you know inside and out? That's the kind of benchmark we're talking about! The "seat time" assessment method complements the "all you can eat" buffet perspective, suggesting it is a quantitative and not qualitative effort that counts. You may have been doing all 1000 questions with the same nasty test-taking habits. For many students, the quantitative approach at least contains a germ of truth - the longer one spends preparing, the more one is likely to learn and understand. Nonetheless, there are two kinds of people on exam day - those who will be able to look in the mirror and know they did everything they could to really learn the material and those who try to convince themselves they did.

C. SAMPLE SCHEDULE – TWO MONTHS AWAY

GOALS, TO DO, and FOLLOW-UP:

Day #1:

GOALS: Practice Reading Critically

TO DO: 50 Multiple choice questions - focus on key words (circle or underline the key words in each question).

FOLLOW-UP: Review questions, reading the outlines about the particular rules raised in the questions if helpful for a deeper understanding; make note cards (see if words circled were appropriately selected). Write out rules learned and highlight the anchor words from rules.

OUTPUT: Review the featured rules, course areas of the day.

Day #2:

GOALS: (1) Learn Evidence Rule: Impeachment by Convictions (and compare it to impeachment by prior untruthful act); create examples of each; (2) Learn Contracts Framework.

TO DO: Do 30 Evidence multiple choice questions; 10 random questions for speed; write essay answer for 45 minutes; review.

FOLLOW-UP: Review all questions for wrong answers, review impeachment convictions with examples and exceptions. Write note cards of rules when appropriate. Recapture rules from day #1.

Day #3:

GOALS: (1) Learn Torts Rule: Negligence per se and compare to *res ipsa*; create examples of each; (2) Learn the Constitutional Law Framework.

TO DO: Say the rules learned out loud; Compare; write pertinent essay answer for 45 minutes. Review; do note cards & review essay; compare to state rules.

FOLLOW-UP: Review; do 20 varied multiple choice questions for speed; do 15 questions asking why the wrong answers are wrong. Identify one big reading issue you have, if any and how to minimize that error. Identify one big thinking issue you have, if any, and how to minimize that issue. Practice doing 10 multiple choice questions focusing solely on your reading and thinking habits. Identify one big writing issue you have and how to minimize that issue. Practice writing for 20 minutes. Review and recapture rules from days 1 - 3.

Day #4:

GOALS: Learn featured Contracts rules about firm offers and modification; compare U.C.C. and common law. Review the Evidence framework.

TO DO: 40 multiple choice questions in Evidence and Contracts; Review for reading skill and why the wrong answers are wrong. Write an essay answer for 40 minutes. Review that answer.

FOLLOW-UP: Review all questions and essays for deep understanding of the rules. Recapture the featured rules of days 1 - 3.

Day #5:

GOALS: Learn featured rules – Learn the Procedural and Substantive Due Process. Compare the two rules; Learn the Property Framework.

TO DO: Do 67 questions for speed; state any rules learned out loud. Make note cards of additional rules learned.

FOLLOW-UP: Review 20 multiple choice questions for key words; review course frameworks; review rules from days 1-4. Identify 1 big reading issue; 1 big thinking issue; and 1 big writing issue. Examine how you are dealing with each issue. Review some major rules in all six Multistate subjects.

Day #6:

GOALS: Learn featured rules - Easements, Licenses, and Profits; compare the three; create examples for each, especially in three areas, creation, scope and termination.

TO DO: Create note cards with the rules learned; do 40 multiple choice questions for reading and speed; Write essay "question asked" and introductions in Property for 4 different questions; rewrite 2 paragraphs for each of the essays written earlier that week. Learn overview hearsay and *Miranda* rules.

FOLLOW-UP: Review multiple choice questions for frameworks, read essay responses out loud; Review and recapture rules from days #1-5.

Day #7:

GOALS: Review all rules covered to date; biggest reading, thinking and writing issues and create strategies for improvement. Plan for next week.

TO DO: Review rules and frameworks of the week (1-3 hours). Plan for next week. Rest! (See a movie.)

D. SAMPLE SCHEDULE – TWO WEEKS AWAY

Day #1:

GOALS: Learn deeply and review Negligence, Landowner's responsibilities; Standards of care; Negligence short-cuts (e.g. negligence per se); Defenses; Murder Types; Mortgages; Character Evidence review; corresponding state law rules.

TO DO: 100 multiple choice questions - simulation under time pressure in a foreign environment, just like the actual exam. State rules and frameworks out loud; write essay for 40 minutes, review (read out loud).

FOLLOW-UP: Review the 100 questions for why the wrong answers are wrong. Make note cards of new rules or strategies learned. Review major rules in all six Multistate subjects.

Day #2:

GOALS: Learn and/or Review Intentional Torts; Co-owners of Property; the First Amendment; Commerce Clause; any corresponding state law rules; the Property and Criminal Law frameworks.

TO DO: 50 multiple choice questions, for key words and frameworks, write an essay answer for 40 minutes, review (read out loud). Make note cards for new rules.

FOLLOW-UP: Review the multiple choice questions for why the wrong answers are wrong. Review the rules learned in the past two weeks. Review strategies for Contracts and Property Law questions. Review state law for Wills and Trusts and UCC, if pertinent.

Day #3:

GOALS: Review Strict Liability; Estates in Land; Dormant Commerce Clause, Privileges and Immunities Clauses; Unilateral Contracts; Hearsay.

TO DO: 50 multiple choice questions with critical reading under time pressure.

FOLLOW-UP: State out loud why the correct answers are correct. Review strategies for Criminal Law and Procedure questions on both the Multistate and State law parts.

Day #4:

GOALS: Review Future Interests; Executive Powers; Breach of Contract issues; the Torts and Constitutional Law frameworks; and state law.

TO DO: 50 multiple choice questions; write 1 essay answer for 60 minutes; review (read out loud).

FOLLOW-UP: Review major rules in all six Multistate subjects.

Day #5:

GOALS: Review Contract remedies; Equal Protection; Contracts and Criminal Procedure frameworks.

TO DO: 30 Qs; write 1 essay answer, 60 minutes; review (read out loud)

FOLLOW-UP: Review strategies for Evidence and Constitutional Law question on both Multistate and State parts of the exam.

Day #6:

GOALS: Review the week's work. Rewrite parts of essays written earlier in the week. Compare rules; compare common law and state law.

Day #7:

GOALS: Review rules and strategies from week.

TO DO: Review trouble spots; review biggest reading, thinking and writing issues. Review strategies for each course (e.g., How will you answer questions in each course?); review all course frameworks; TAKE A BREAK!

VI. <u>TECHNIQUES FOR SUCCESS</u>

Chapter Points
(1) Learn Course and Question Frameworks.
(2) Practice Reading Critically: Studying the Right Way.

A. FRAMEWORKS AND PROTOCOLS: LEARN A DANCE, NOT A POSE

1. *Frameworks and Protocols – Travel Maps for Courses and Legal Rules*

"Fear causes hesitation, and hesitation will cause your worst fears to come true."– Point Break, 1992

Get a concise process and stick to it.

   Let's face it. Sometimes the best answers to complex questions are very simple. One very common problem for bar takers is that they get over-paranoid and assume that an obvious answer must be a trick answer. This is perhaps the worst trick of all. Because some of the bar exam questions are very difficult and sometimes tricky and many bar classes teach you to be wary of obvious answers, you may start fighting your own instincts. At the very least, it's important to remember one simple rule - your first instinct may often be right. Although some of the more difficult questions may require deep rule analysis, you must have the confidence to trust yourself. If you hesitate too much, you may find yourself haunted by two answers you can't seem to choose between. The best way to avoid agonizing over an obvious answer and a tricky answer is to know the rules and elements and understand them.

   Now, we've come up with a way for you to "FRAME" different subjects and then follow specific "protocols" on how to analyze a question. These things map out the courses and rules in precise steps. The steps for the waltz are different from the steps for the tango. You need to similarly distinguish between the steps for different legal rules, such as the Privileges and Immunities Clause of Article IV and the Dormant Commerce Clause. That's what we're going to go over in this chapter. We've given you the lengthy speeches, the pep rally and the suggested schedules - now we're going to start teaching you how to analyze bar exam style questions. Just to give you a global view of what we're about to cover, here's a quick overview:

How to Analyze Bar Exam Questions

(1) Use a funnel: Start large, and then go small.

(2) Identify the course and subject matter.

(3) Apply the frameworks to pinpoint the issue with multiple choice questions.

(4) Eliminate wrong answers to get the best answer.

(5) With essays, answer the specific question asked, and follow a protocol in framing your answers.

OK, **READY?** *Here we go.*

Why Protocols?

The short answer is that most experts use them. If you were a patient and had to go see a doctor, the doctor wouldn't just grab the scalpel and operate, would she? Well, let's hope not. If she does, we recommend you find medical assistance elsewhere! Nonetheless, the doctor would have a "framework" on how to examine you (first, look you over visually, then use the stethoscope and ask you to say "ah," check your blood pressure and ask you a series of questions). If it's helpful, she'll also take an x-ray. Okay, we're going to give you a framework system for analyzing bar exam questions. Each applicable rule in a bar question has its own set of protocols. The protocols would be the next step after you apply your course framework. Let's turn our attention back to the medical example.

After doctors do their initial diagnosis by applying their medical "framework," they (hypothetically) will make a determination of what's wrong. Let's say it's a possible bacterial infection from a cut you got while swimming. Okay, what's the protocol for a bacterial infection? It may be, first, make sure the wound isn't already infected, then dress the wound and give the patient an antibiotic. (Remember, we went to law school, so don't try this at home.) Let's take a look at the basic framework of Constitutional Law.

CONSTITUTIONAL LAW

POWERS   LIMITS

Federal
State

Legislative -
Executive - Judicial

First Amendment –
        Speech and Religion
Due Process
Equal Protection
Dormant Commerce Clause
Privileges and Immunities
Clauses
Contracts Clause
Takings Clause
Tenth Amendment

Constitutional law is broken down into two kinds of questions – those that deal with governmental powers and those that deal with limits that protect the individual from the government. What's an example of a governmental power? Well, how about the president's power to pardon someone accused of a *federal* crime? That power is vested in Article II of the Constitution and cannot be challenged or revoked by the courts or Congress. Here's another power – Congress' power to declare war. That power is vested in Article I of the Constitution. Those are examples of powers.

Now, let's look at some limits because that's what James Madison said was needed when he wrote the Bill of Rights. In fact, the Constitution was initially designed to protect the people from the federal government. It was only well after the 14th Amendment was enacted that the Supreme Court concluded the Bill of Rights that are fundamental to our American scheme of liberty and are incorporated through the 14th Amendment's Due Process Clause and apply to the states. The 14th Amendment's Due Process Clause applies to the states, but the 5th Amendment's Due Process Clause applies only to the federal government. The point is this – one fast-acting limit, due process, includes a lot of rules you have to know, including substantive due process, the right to refuse medical treatment, void for vagueness and, as discussed below, procedural due process. Yes, it does get complicated.

No Shortcuts:
Use powers-limits to frame most constitutional analysis

Procedural Due Process Protocol

Steps:
(1) Is there a government deprivation of life, liberty or property?
(2) (a) If NO: No violation of due process.
(2) (b) If YES: Apply the *Matthews* balancing test of

interests to see if the petitioner is entitled to notice or a hearing or both.

Do you see how we did that? Let's check it out. You're taking the bar exam in that big warehouse of a room. The guy next to you is freaking out and that's freaking you out. You're on question 87 and can't wait to get that long deserved lunch break. All you can seem to think about is a cheeseburger and a cool vanilla shake. Hey, we understand. But get that cheeseburger out of your mind and focus! And stop freaking out because you've got something that guy next to you doesn't have - the frameworks and the protocols. Here we go. It's question 87. The question involves a woman who was just denied her right to collect her welfare benefits. It will probably look something like this:

87. Monica's roommate, Rachel, has been a resident of the state of Gain for five years. Unfortunately, Rachel just lost her job at the local coffee shop as a counter-person. Determined not to use her father's credit cards to survive, she's applied for unemployment/welfare benefits from the state of Gain. After filling out an application and making all the appropriate filings at the local state unemployment office, Rachel eagerly waited for her unemployment check. Rachel received 5 checks over the next several months. Then Rachel got a post-card from an unidentified government employee, which simply told her that her claims were no longer considered valid and that her checks were being discontinued immediately. When Rachel tried to call and ask why, she was refused an answer; the government employee then simply hung up. When she called back and requested a hearing, she was told that under Gain state law she wasn't entitled to one. The checks stopped coming.

89

What is Rachel's <u>best</u> argument that she has been deprived of her constitutional rights?

(A) The discontinued checks violated her rights under the 14th Amendment Equal Protection Clause because of obvious government discrimination.
(B) Her 14th Amendment right to Due Process was violated because of a deprivation of a property interest.
(C) Rachel is entitled to benefits under the Privileges and Immunities Clause of Art. IV as a resident of the state.
(D) Rachel was denied her 'Right to Work' under the state constitution of Gain.

<u>Multiple Choice Question Protocol</u>

Here's how the multiple choice question protocol applies to the question you just did, Question 87.

Part 1: Read the Call of the Question <u>Critically</u>
- What words with legal inferences do you see? *Deprived of her constitutional rights.*
- What Course Are You In? *Constitutional Law*
- What does the call of the question ask for? Here, it is *the <u>best</u> argument that plaintiff has been denied her constitutional rights.*
- Who is Rachel? *Plaintiff or Petitioner.*

Part 2: Skim the Answer Choices for the <u>Location</u> of the Course
- Apply the Framework: Is this question about governmental powers or limits? *Limits.*
- What kind of limits are being offered as answer choices? *Equal Protection, Privileges and Immunities,*

Procedural Due Process (PDP) and the state 'Right to Work'.

Part 3: **Read the Fact Pattern in a <u>Directed</u> Fashion**

- What words of legal significance do you see? *How about benefits, notice and a hearing?*
- What important facts do you see? *Rachel has been receiving benefits from the government. The benefits were cut off without a stated reason.*

Part 4: **Eliminate <u>Wrong</u> Answer Choices**

(C) This is not about discrimination against an out-of-state resident, so the Privileges and Immunities Clause is not an issue.

(D) Rachel isn't being denied her right to <u>work</u>; she was denied her right to be heard.

Part 5: **Apply the Protocols to Pick the <u>Right </u>Answer**

(A) Apply the Protocol for Equal Protection
Was there Government discrimination against a group? (Look for race, alienage OR national origin, OR gender or non-marital children status.) *No*

(B) Apply the Protocol for PDP
- Was there government deprivation of life, liberty or property? *Yes – a property interest, an entitlement to unemployment benefits created by state law*
- What process is due? *Balance interests*
- *Matthews* balancing test – get notice or hearing or both

Part 6: **Re-Read the Call for the Question to Pick the Right Answer Choice**

The call of the question asked for Rachel's *best* argument. Choice (B) *is the better answer choice.* (Look for the "better" answer instead of the absolutely best answer ever.)

Move on to the next question with confidence: don't look back

Here's another important tip. It's very common for bar-takers to let a difficult question haunt them throughout the exam. Often times, your first instinct is right and you've made it safely to Hawaii. If you have confidence, you won't let doubt get you on the Red-eye back to Las Vegas. It's often very bad to change answers for a variety of reasons. For one, the MBE is done on a Scantron sheet that is being graded by a machine. As you well know, Scantron machines gobble up No. 2 lead. If you've erased an answer incompletely and the machine senses your first answer and your new answer, it will assume you've marked two answers for the same question and automatically mark the question wrong. Although you can pay seven dollars to the graders (American College Testing (ACT)) to hand-grade your exam afterwards, it is extremely unlikely that your re-grade will come back as you hope. Unless you marked the wrong answer choice for the wrong question (answering question 32 in the answer 33 bubble), just move on.

2. Essay Questions

Essay questions are a little different than multiple choice questions because they're specifically framed. In other words, most of the time, you'll be able to identify fairly quickly what the MAIN subject area of law you're in. If it's a dispute between the owner of Whiteacre and Blackacre, it's most likely Property. (There may be another subject area tucked in there somewhere that deserves some attention, but for the most part, the question will focus on one primary area of law.)

But, it is really important to figure out where to go once you are in that course - and not to note-dump or outline-dump like you might have done in law school. The exam graders just don't have the time - or likely the patience - to sift through your outline on a subject to pick out the hidden gems.

The typical essay reader is grading hundreds of tests and is looking for specific things. The typical essay gets read quickly. Our point? Streamline. Don't put unnecessary information in there and weigh the reader down with superfluous stuff - just because it was in an outline. It's certainly fine to throw reasonable guesses out there. Just remember not to talk about what you want - write about what the GRADER wants. Here's a set of specific tips to remember:

> *Answer the question the examiners ask –*
> *not the one you want to answer*

A. Answer the question that was asked, the legal question that was asked in the hypothetical. Don't stray. Most of the time, the question you are asked will involve a lawsuit involving two or more parties (A v. B) and as an inquiry, should end with a question mark.

B. Make sure to make a statement describing the elements of the applicable rules. When students state the rules, they often skim and don't include all of the elements, but that's a mistake because that's what frames the analysis to come and gets you points.

C. Make sure to apply each element using separate paragraphs for each element. Don't jam it all into one paragraph.

D. Don't forget your conclusion, but remember not to be too firm by jumping strongly to one side as opposed to another. (Using words such as "likely" or "probably" is perfectly acceptable.)

3. Whole Rule Analysis

"Whole Rule Analysis" is a protocol or method for understanding rules. The goal of understanding is not just to know the words of the rule, but also to know what they mean, to give examples and do comparisons. It's asking whether you understand a particular element. For example, unless you can compare negligence per se and *res ipsa*, murder and felony murder, licenses and easements, the Dormant Commerce Clause and the regular Commerce Clause and the difference between the Privileges and Immunities Clauses in Article IV and the 14th Amendment, you're going to miss some serious points.

For instance, an easement is:

(1) The right to use another's land, and is generally
(1) In writing and
(2) Irrevocable.

A license is:

(1) The right to use another's land but can be
(2) Oral and
(3) Is generally revocable.

Reviewing the similarities and differences between licenses and easements is very helpful to effective studying. Both negligence per se and *res ipsa* are negligence shortcuts. Negligence per se requires a statutory violation and *res ipsa loquitur* involves an inference of negligence from the circumstances. Murder is the unlawful killing of another human being with malice. Felony murder is the killing of a human being during the commission of a felony or an attempted felony. Let's break murder down a little further to give you an example:

MURDER

1. The Unlawful Killing
2. Of Another Human Being
3. With Malice (aforethought)

    1. Unlawful Killing: A killing that is not justifiable (e.g., not self-defense) or excusable (e.g., not insanity)
    2. Of Another Human Being: It can't be an animal - even if it has personality, like Flipper.
    3. With Malice: To act (a) Purposely, (b) Knowingly or (c) Grossly Recklessly
        a. Purposely: To desire the results.
        b. Knowingly: To act with conscious awareness that the results are practically certain to occur.
        c. Recklessly: To act with conscious disregard of an unreasonable and substantial risk.
        d. Grossly reckless: To act with a gross disregard of an unreasonable and substantial risk. With respect to murder, this means to act with a gross indifference to human life.

4. Funnel It

It's very important to make sure that you really understand a single rule completely, inside and out, just like we did a moment ago with murder. However, it's also important to know where a rule fits in the overall framework of a subject. Think of it as a map or getting directions to a particular restaurant. Let's say you're on your way to the "Bar Exam Restaurant" and someone tells you it's on 1st Avenue. Now, if you live in the same town as the restaurant, it's not that hard to find 1st Avenue. But let's say that the restaurant is in another town somewhere in the county. Going to 1st Avenue isn't going to help you very much unless you know which town it's in. It's the same for subject matter. If someone tells you that you've got a question dealing with "Conspiracy" you know it's in Criminal Law. Conspiracy is like the street name and Criminal Law is the county. But wait a minute. What town is that in? We call it "Inchoate Crimes," and it also houses any attempted crimes as well. Here's another example - "Unlawful Killings of Another."

"Unlawful Killings of Another" is a "town" that houses Murder, Felony Murder, Voluntary and Involuntary Manslaughter. All of these "streets" can be found in the town of "Killings," which is in the county of Criminal Law.

> Use the Funnel:
> Start with the course, then narrow the location to a subject area, then narrow it to a rule and its precise elements.
> Make this your automatic practice.

Here's a quick map:

CRIMINAL LAW

UNLAWFUL KILLING OF ANOTHER PERSON

MURDER
FELONY MURDER
VOLUNTARY MANSLAUGHTER
INVOLUNTARY MANSLAUGHTER

Now, here's a doozy. What if you get a question about attempted murder? Aha! Now you probably want to get in your convertible Corvette (we love convertible Corvettes) and cruise right over to the town of Killings, right? WRONG! This is what we mean. You've GOT to know what towns these streets are in.

You go to Inchoate (incomplete) Crimes. Here's where it fits in:

<u>INCHOATE CRIMES</u>

ATTEMPT
CONSPIRACY
SOLICITATION

5. The Right Direction

Okay, now you've got a pretty good idea where we're going with all this. However, all of this is useless unless you realize that without this kind of analysis, you're going in the wrong direction. It's good to get a study partner or even a bar tutor to get regular feedback on a timely basis. When people train for a competitive sport, they get a coach, right? What makes you think studying for the bar exam is any different? It's not. Whether you're getting the right answer or the wrong answer, it's not as important as to whether or not you're guessing or applying the proper framework and protocols to the question. To fix a problem, you've got to identify it first. You wouldn't take your Corvette into an auto shop and let a mechanic simply guess at what's wrong, would you? (Okay, we admit, this is probably an accurate version of what happens, but let's pretend it's a perfect world.)

What you really want, of course, is for a skilled mechanic to inspect your engine and diagnose it. That's what we want you to do. Be a skilled bar exam mechanic and diagnose the question like an engine. You've got to know *why* you're getting a question wrong. Was it merely a failure to critically read something correctly? Did you forget to notice that the question mentioned the word "attempt" somewhere and you jumped to the "Unlawful Killings" framework instead of going correctly to "Inchoate Crimes?" Was it a lack of whole rule analysis? Did you analyze a murder and forget what the specific term for "purposeful" is under the "malice" part of the rule?

VII. <u>CRITICAL READING TECHNIQUES</u>

Chapter Points
(1) Learn to Actively Read.
(2) Identify Important Words.
(3) Identify the Real Issues.

A. PRACTICE READING CRITICALLY: APPLY ACTIVE STUDYING TECHNIQUES

> *"When I make a word do a lot of work like that,*
> *I always pay it extra."*
> *- Lewis Carroll (1832-1898) [Through the Looking Glass]*

> *Question by New York City Tourist:*
> *"Excuse me, but how do you get to Carnegie Hall?"*
> *Answer: "Practice, Practice, Practice." – Anonymous*

Just like in law school, there are different levels of advancement in the bar exam study process. Instead of being a 1L, 2L or 3L, however, you'll have to be honest enough with yourself on where you stand in terms of preparation readiness and proficiency. There are always going to be certain people who only know one way to prepare for a test, and it may be difficult for them to "rocket up to the next level."

While students who fail may advance only incrementally on the scoring chart, the goal is simple – to fly past the score requirement, safely into the passing zone. That flight often takes different techniques and strategies. The techniques listed below are designed to give you this extra lift.

Critical Reading Means Thinking While Reading

Critical reading involves extracting the legal issues and how to solve them from the facts, the responses (if multiple choice), and the calls of the question. Critical reading means the reader is thinking while reading actively distinguishing important words from background context, exam directions from facts, words that have potential legal ramifications from those that do not. If the reading is inaccurate, or the reader simply fails to spot and identify important words or phrases, the skills of thinking and writing will be minimized or rendered moot.

Although critical reading is, well, critical, a lot of people seem to blow it off. They simply let their eyes glaze over the material. You know, you're looking at the page but you're not really paying attention. You're thinking about ice cream, that cute guy or gal you saw last week at the local watering-hole, or trying to figure out what really happened to the missing 18 minutes of the Watergate tapes. Okay, maybe you're not too worried about that last one, but it's always possible. Our point is that you're distracted! Are you even reading this book at this point? After 5 chapters, you're probably thinking, c'mon guys! I'm sick of all of this bar exam nonsense.

The more you tune in, the more likely you are to stay tuned. The more you train your brain to be lazy, the more it will want to take it easy. The old saying that "fuzzy writing is a reflection of fuzzy thinking" should be modified to "fuzzy critical reading may lead to fuzzy thinking and writing."

Fuzzy Critical Reading May Lead to Fuzzy Thinking and Writing

On bar exam questions, like law school exams, some words work harder than others. The reason some words matter more than others for resolving questions relates to critical reading. Reading critically is the gateway to legal reasoning and problem solving. The natural sequence when taking a test is to read, think and act (usually write), although the three components really blend in with each other when working properly.

The Sequence: Read – Think – Act – Write

A lot of people pass right on by critical reading when preparing for the bar exam. This is a big mistake, however, because "trigger words" help you spot the issue. Identifying issues, and judging which issues are the best ones to negotiate, is a really important skill that will help you take command of the exam. Reading critically isn't something that's "hardwired" in most students. Instead, critical reading takes practice and effort. Once you start, you'll be hot on the trail and good to go. Just give yourself a chance. You may actually start enjoying your learning process.

Remember: on the bar exam, some words work harder than others.

OK, **READY**? *Here we go.*

1. Step #1: *Understanding that Not All Words are Created Equal*

It's important to recognize that certain words in a multiple choice or essay question are more important than others. The mere recognition of critical reading is a move in the right direction. The more important words include the pivotal facts, the key parts of the call of the question and the assertions of the options. All of these words, in the eyes of Lewis Carroll, work overtime.

2. Step #2: *Spotting Important Words*

It's also important to spot these words and understand what they infer. This combination of thinking-while-reading can be critical to solving whatever problem you're presented with by the examiners. For example, the statement "Jones slipped and fell on the sidewalk right where Adam had dropped his banana peel" has immediate implications in the law; so does the statement "Barbara was asked while testifying during cross-examination whether she had ever been convicted of grand theft auto." Both of these statements yield legal issues that can be discussed and analyzed by students. Many students, however, gloss over the salient words in the statements, lumping all of the words together. Instead, Jones' slip and fall on a banana peel should be related to a possible tort and the cross-examination of Barbara reveals a likely impeachment issue in Evidence.

Critical reading isn't just a mental exercise. There are a lot of forms of what we call "corollary writing." Lots of students make notes as they read, and this counts too. Even underlining is a form of critical writing. But it does not count if they underline everything that is, they highlight or underline every single word in the fact patterns (the stimulus of the question). This isn't going to help much because if you underline *everything* you can't determine what's important and what's not. In reality, it's no different than if they hadn't underlined anything at all! The keep-it-clean students maintain their exams as "new" and attempt to spot the legal significance of words and analyze solely by keeping a mental file on them.

One skill associated with reading critically is "translation," discussed in greater detail below. Translation is a significant first step toward answering fact-based questions.

3. Technique #1: Practice Translation

Translation means drawing legal inferences from facts.

"Translation" is a skill used to draw helpful legal inferences from the facts of a problem. Because translation is a skill, it can be practiced and refined. Translation is just one way to seek reading clues from words in the question and is a description of what is commonly referred to as "issue-spotting." Okay, now you're on board with us, right? If you've heard anything about the bar exam or even recall that phrase from law school, "issue-spotting" is pretty self-explanatory. This technique, however, is larger than simply spotting the issue in a question, reaching further to include a general orientation toward evaluating the *value of all words* in the context of a question. The key to this skill is understanding that some words become important by virtue of context and other words have significance almost regardless of context. In essence, not all words are created equal.

All too often, people study by reading the rules of law and then illustrations of how those rules are applied. Rarely do students practice by focusing on a crucial aspect of both multiple choice and essay-type questions – the facts – and attempting to improve their "translation" ability. If you're a bit confused, don't worry, because we're about to explain ourselves in further detail. The following paragraphs offer several techniques on how to engage in effective "translation."

Step #1 – It definitely helps while analyzing multiple choice questions to mentally place the words you're reading into one of three categories.

Three Categories of Words
(1) Background Words
(2) Words of Important Legal Significance
(3) Words of Important Test-Taking Significance

Each question on the exam includes some background words, providing context, nuance and a story to the problem at hand. However, there are some words that have legal significance. By this, we mean, they relate to legal rules, defenses, and causes of action. Examples are "objection", which relates to trial and evidence law and "defendants," which also relates to trials, evidence, and other subject areas. The word "agreement" has great significance in contract law. The phrase "Congress passed a law" has great significance in constitutional law. The words of potential legal significance should be connected to the particular rule, element, defense, or cause of action by the good test taker. The skill of translation is really a large part of critical reading. When a good reader reads a word of legal significance, the reader will make that notation in her mind (and often then on paper). A poor reader, on the other hand, will simply skim over the words, not grasping the entire significance of them.

> *Some test-taking words:*
> *"Because", "if", "unless", "provided that"*

The same skill is required for "interpreting" the significance of test-taking words. In most multiple choice question responses, a conclusion is given first, such as "A will win," and then an important test-taking word will follow, such as "because," "if" or "unless." These words – "because," "if," "unless" – are critical to unraveling the focus and propriety of each answer choice. Thus, if an answer choice reads something to the effect of, "A will win, unless the contract provides for a condition subsequent," the word "unless" has critical significance in understanding the truthfulness and accuracy of the response. The word "unless" really changes the answer choice so that instead of saying, "A will win", it means "B will win if...." Good test-takers look for these words and immediately understand the role they play in the question. Poor test-takers skim over these words and look at the answer choice as a whole, failing to categorize and highlight the particular words in question.

One way to practice identifying words with legal significance is to select words in fact patterns and "draw" legal issue inference chains, either out loud or in writing, from the word or phrase. An example is the word "defamation," which has legal significance in several areas of evidence law (character and hearsay), torts (a type of tort) and constitutional law (unprotected speech). Another word with legal significance is "mistake," which has multiple meanings in criminal law, serving to negate the mental state of a crime or as part of a legitimate affirmative defense to a crime.

> Practice by drawing legal issue
> inference chains.

A different way of identifying words with legal significance is recognizing words that often trigger particular legal issues. This proactive form of studying is a way to identify the types of facts that yield certain legal issues. While not always accurate, this technique provides a way to actively read and evaluate facts at the same time. In addition, the test-taker can more plainly see how facts are really legal issue triggers. Here are some examples:

> *Facts that create legal issues*

FACT PATTERN	TRIGGERED LEGAL ISSUE
Congress regulates selling	Commerce Clause Powers
Cutting through the neighbor's backyard	Easements or licenses
Tickets to plays, films, or events	Licenses
State laws	Police Powers
State laws regulating transportation, buying or selling	Dormant Commerce Clause
State law regulating citizens of other states while in the state	Privileges and Immunities Clause of Article IV

Asking witness questions on cross-examination	Impeachment
Dead Body	Homicide
Party statements	Admissions

The final word category of translation includes words of exam-taking significance, or leverage words. Leverage words are those words in the options or call that significantly affect whether the option is the key – the correct response – or merely a distractor. First tier leverage words exist in almost all of the questions and are those words that dictate the structure of the option – whether it has an explanation and, if so, in what form. These words include "because," "if," "unless," "but only," and similar directives. For example,

Will X win?

A. Yes, because....
B. Yes, if....
C. No, unless....
D. No, because....

The "yes" and "no" parts of the answers are less important than the leverage words that follow. It is helpful practice to do multiple choice questions focusing on the leverage words. This strategy will yield a better understanding of the questions and, consequently, a better opportunity to distinguish the correct from incorrect answer choices. Roughly translated, you've got to get a grip on leverage words and phrases. There's a huge difference between "Yes, because" and "Yes, if." The word "if" means that the answer is an exception, depending on the circumstances that follow the "if." On the other hand, the "No, unless" really means "yes, if ...."

Practice Method: Reading ONLY the call of the question and then skimming the options for 10 seconds maximum, practice identifying the leverage words. Then, draw inferences from facts and infer legal issues, rules and consequences.

4. Technique #2: Identifying "Real" Issues

This technique applies to critical writing as well as to critical thinking. It's pretty common for students to describe the issue in a question as one relating to an entire legal rule, such as "murder" or "*res ipsa loquitur*," when the "real" issue is a subset of the elements of the legal rule, such as malice or a rebuttable inference of negligence, respectively. Remember how we talked about "Whole Rule Analysis?" Well, that's what we're talking about now. The following multiple choice question elaborates on the *res ipsa loquitur* example, showing that the way students remember the rule as "the thing speaks for itself" is not tremendously useful in unlocking the "real" issue in precise and deep bar questions.

> *Question*: Johnnie, a traveling salesman, was staying at the Holiday Inn near Indianapolis. It was a bit stuffy in his room and he decided to open a window. The crank window had a handle, which was a bit loose from use. When Johnnie cranked the handle hard, he heard a whoosh and the pane of glass came out and broke around him, cutting his hand in several places. The manufacturer of the window, the Wonder Window Company, had installed a new kind of cheaper handle on the window. Few problems had been reported about the new, less expensive handle.
>
> Johnnie filed a negligence action against the Wonder Window Company for damages. The Company claimed it was not negligent. Johnnie bases his claim on a theory of *res ipsa loquitur*. Will he win?

A. Yes, because a glass window will never break because of a problematic handle.

B. Yes, because the window was not within Johnnie's dominion and control.

C. No, unless the window was within the control of Wonder Window Co.

D. No, if others who had used the handle prior to Johnnie had destabilized the window.

The key is choice D. The first observation to make is that the "yes-yes" "no-no" components of the responses are not dispositive of which answer choice is the key and which are the distractors. While other options are in some ways appealing, they all contain defects. Answer choice A is appealing and reflects the res ipsa loquitur theory upon which this suit is based, but does not approach the "real" issue here – the fact that in *res ipsa loquitur*, the inference of negligence is rebuttable. Remember, "if" is a powerful word – and it's always something you want to pay very close attention to when reading the answer choices.

ILLUSTRATIONS

The following questions demonstrate how to apply critical reading techniques, using reading to glean important information, specifically about the legal issues. The critical reading incorporates the skills of translation and looking for issue triggers.

> *Question 1. Florida law: "No resident alien living in Florida may receive mental health benefits unless the person has resided in the state for more than two years." Is this law constitutional?*

Students should see that words like "alien" and "resident alien" make a difference in constitutional law. Any law that classifies, such as this one, which classifies based on alienage, may indeed trigger equal protection clause analysis. Further, the fact that benefits are restricted to individuals who resided in the state for a certain length of time triggers the implied fundamental right to travel as well. Thus, this brief law is chock full of legal implications. Seeing them all requires critical reading.

> *Question 2. <u>Alabama law</u>: "No tenured teachers at state universities may receive health and other benefits after the age of 50." Is the law constitutional?*

Here again, the question involves a law, which indicates there may be a constitutional issue. The law denies tenured teachers health and other benefits after the age of 50, classifying based on age, again creating an equal protection clause analysis. The deprivation of benefits triggers another area of the Constitution, namely procedural due process. If tenured teachers had a legitimate claim of entitlement to such benefits, a due process analysis may be appropriate.

> *Question 3. Which of the following is least likely to create a successful nuisance action?*

A. Brooke decides to raise little pigs in her backyard in the middle of a beautiful downtown of a western metropolis.
B. Paola waters her lawn and regularly sprays the yard next to hers, ruining her neighbor's outdoor furniture.
C. Ryan regularly builds a huge bonfire on the side of his house, creating mounds of smoke that suffocate the neighborhood.
D. Jessica always practices her opera singing when she comes home from work five days a week, most often at 4:00 a.m. Her singing regularly wakes the neighbors and their pet animals.

Critical Reading Techniques

The key to reading multiple choice questions critically is to understand not only what the body of the question yields but also the answer choices – which truly dictate the nature of the question. The key to this problem are the words "least likely," which talk about the worst argument available in a context of nuisance. For starters, you've got to really understand what nuisance means, from which area of the law it comes from to its limits. In this problem, although you may have flown right past it, the call of the question asked you to determine when there is a use of one's property creating a substantial and unreasonable non-trespassory interference with the use and enjoyment of another's property. Thus, answer "B" is the worst answer (which here is the correct answer) because it is a trespassory invasion of the neighbor's yard, as compared to a non-trespassory interference such as "C" and "D." "A" is also not the correct answer, given the context of raising pigs in a beautiful urban neighborhood.

Question 4. Allan has lived next door to Arturo for 26 years. Unbeknownst to Allan, his fence has extended over his property line and onto Arturo's property by two feet during that time. If Arturo goes to sell his own property and learns about the true placement of the fence, what is the consequence of the fence being misplaced for all of those years?

A. Allan now owns two feet of Arturo's property, regardless of whether he thought he was adversely possessing it or not.

B. Allan now owns one foot of Arturo's property under the common law "split the difference" rule of decision of disputed property.

C. Allan does not own any of Arturo's property because Allan did not know that Arturo adversely possessed it.

D. Allan has a fence easement, which permits him to maintain the fence on the disputed property.

When a fact pattern indicates there's an issue between neighbors, several potential legal issues may result. Nuisance is one possible issue that occurs, and another is adverse possession. The issue here appears to be adverse possession because it concerns a persistent trespass on another's property. (Answer choice "A" reflects the law of adverse possession.) However, a key to reading critically here is also seeing that there was a dispute between neighbors. In addition to adverse possession and nuisance, the fact that neighbors are involved indicates there could also be easement, license, or profit issues that result, as well as negative restrictive covenants.

> *Question 5. Adjia phones Zenia and says, "I will rent to you my Hutchinson Island house for two years at $400 per month." Zenia accepts. Zenia has*:

A. A tenancy for years.
B. A tenancy at will.
C. A periodic tenancy.
D. No tenancy at all.

The key word or words in this particular problem appear to be the length of time, which is what we italicized for you. But, aha! We tricked you. The key word is "phones." *What?!* Yeah, that's right, the key word is "phones." Before you get all bent out of shape, check it out! The reason why that word is so important is it indicates there was an oral conversation between Adjia and Zenia, undermining the lease agreement, which is subject to the statute of frauds and must be in writing. For students who blithely read over that word and simply focus on the nature of the agreement, they miss the essence of the question. Keep an eye out for those kinds of reading challenges. The bar examiners love to play around that way.

VIII. <u>CRITICAL THINKING TECHNIQUES</u>

Chapter Points:
(1) Learn Techniques, Don't Just "Do Problems".
(2) Thinking is About Output – Not Just Input.
(3) Make Sure Your Studying is "Useful for the Bar Exam"
 – Make That Your Mantra.

A. CRITICAL THINKING TECHNIQUES

It can be helpful to practice critical thinking techniques beyond reading outlines of black letter law and doing mass quantities of practice multiple choice questions.

It is how you do the questions that matters, not just doing larger quantities. The key is using techniques. One technique focuses on the protocols for analyzing questions within courses or doctrinal subjects – what each course essentially means in a quick and easy visual chart. Another technique is learning the words that trigger different issues, such as production manufacturing and transportation laws by states, triggering the Dormant Commerce Clause, or laws discriminating against residents of other states, triggering the Privileges and Immunities Clause of Article IV Section 2. You can actually study these triggers just as much as you can study the elements of causes of action and defenses or exceptions in learning rules and principles.

1. Technique #1: Aim for Mastery

Mastery means thorough knowledge of a rule and how to apply it. A rule has to be accessible and revealed by output – can you write it all down or say it out loud? Your knowledge must be concise enough to use in 1.8 minutes (for multiple choice questions) and almost as fast for essays. Learn the anchor words – words that open up the whole area. For example, anchor words in the Evidence exclusion Offers to Compromise include a (1) prerequisite (a dispute in validity or amount) and (2) a partial exclusion (offers, compromises and negotiation). In felony murder, an anchor word is "killing" because felony murder requires a killing during a felony or attempted felony, not a "murder" during a felony or attempted felony. Anchor words are those essential words to know in describing a concept for its content or method.

Instead of studying one course at a time or one doctrine at a time, it is best to set one's sights on immediacy – the rule or rules for the day. This rules-based learning seeks mastery, not coverage, and is based on the premise that a little learned about a lot of subjects is often ineffective for the pointed and deep questions on the bar exam – particularly the Multistate multiple choice item types. What we're talking about here is whole rule analysis. You need to have the confidence that you have mastered whole rule analysis, and the only way to do that is to master output, not just input. You need to be able to not only comprehend the rules you studied but be able to recite them verbally, aloud. Very few students will do this, but the ones that master output will be able to recite every element to the rules they've studied and it will help them significantly on the exam.

2. Technique #2: Funnel

> Funneling to locate rules and
> issues is an important
> prerequisite to application.

No Shortcuts! Too many students start with the rule or parts of a rule, instead of from the beginning – (1) which course? Only then can it be asked, (2) which subject area? And then, (3) what are the elements of the pertinent rule? And then, (4) what do those elements mean? The key to the "funnel" approach is that even when a rule is learned, students should still keep starting with the course.....the same way all of the time. No shortcuts!

With the overwhelming quantity of information unleashed by the bar exam, it is easy to lose sight of the forest for all of the trees. When prepping, students should make sure they label the particular forest – really, course – each rule is from. For example, instead of diving right in to understand all of the elements of *res ipsa loquitur*, it may be a helpful reminder that the rule is part of negligence and yields a "shortcut" to proof.

Example: *Res Ipsa*

Funnel:
1. Torts
2. Negligence
3. Shortcut (alternative to Proving duty and breach)
4. Elements
5. Explanations

3. Technique #3: Practice Thinking Out Loud

Thinking is not something that one does entirely inside one's head. It is expressed, either in writing, verbally; or even nonverbally. For the bar exam, too many students do not have any outward expression on a day-to-day basis to see if they are thinking or how that thinking is going. Feedback is important and to get it, there must be practice in critical thinking.

    a.   Analyzing Questions "Out Loud"
    b.   Rules-Based Studying, Not Course-Based
    c.   Dig Deeper

To maintain a feedback loop and determine whether the studying is reaping results, it might be helpful to offer legal analysis out loud. When held up in the open like that, it will be easiest to inspect and evaluate.

4. Technique #4: Make Flash Cards

These aren't the same as the commercial flashcards; these cards should be custom-made to your learning style, very concise and USEABLE FOR THE EXAM. Too many cards are useable for studying, but not the exam. That means cards should have the 4EC's on them, emphasizing anchor words. The "4EC's" refers to the Elements, Explanations, Examples, Exceptions and Comparisons of a rule. Knowing the 4 EC's reflects deep knowledge. For example, murder is (1) the unlawful (2) killing of another person (3) with malice. So there are three elements. Malice in murder means either purpose, knowledge or gross recklessness. An example is purposely killing an enemy. An exception is killing when provoked (heat of passion manslaughter). A comparison is to felony murder.

Don't replicate treatises or bar review books. You already have those books. If you are a visual learner, go ahead and use colors or the like. If you want, draw pictures. Make the cards valuable to you.

a. Learning the Vocabulary of Bar Prep – The Elements

The vocabulary of law covers the elements of causes of action, claims and defenses. The 4EC's provide an expansive understanding of the rule vocabulary – elements, explanations, examples, exceptions (or defenses) and comparisons (to other rules or elements). Preparing your own flash cards of the 4EC's serves dual purposes – it is an active exercise that helps to cement the rule or principle in the test-taker's memory and the card can be used over and over again, to promote enhanced understanding.

5. Technique #5: Make Car Tapes or CD's

One place students often waste time is in their cars, commuting to and from work and traveling on a daily basis. To make such time productive, one option is to create "car tapes," interactive cassette tapes (or CDs).

Studying in the car really means talking out loud – saying rules, repeating protocols, and just plain going over any bar-related material. Yes – still keep your eyes on the road at all times. Listening to bar tapes counts – but to internalize them, stop the tapes or CD's and repeat them. Better yet, make your own tapes with your own voice and pause – so you can talk back in the car.

6. Technique #6: Repetition – Recapturing Rules and Elements

Many people need repetition to learn – including the authors. Some people need dozens or even hundreds of times. Riding a bicycle takes several repetitions. Playing the piano takes longer. Learning a language may take longer or shorter (depending on which language, of course). Give yourself time to repeat – lots.

Given the large amount of rules and principles to learn, it's easy to forget some rules and principles already covered during bar preparations. To make sure the "forgetting principle" does not apply, there must be a conscious effort to retain previously covered rules.

> The "Forgetting Principle" –
> *Knowledge, unless cemented through repetition,
> has a way of disappearing from present memory.*

7. Technique #7: Magic Opening Phrases

One problem facing students involves the retention of what is learned. Without anchoring words or phrases, knowledge gained often floats away and becomes unavailable at the time of the bar exam. Special techniques can be used to promote recall. One useful technique is to remember rules by using the same opening words each time. These "magic words" become the clues or anchors to remembering each and every element of a rule. These opening phrases are the phrases that are the quick "anchoring words" that open the entire definition. They are magic phrases because they are the things to remember that count a lot more than the rest of the definition. The remaining words are not as important and serve to muddy the waters if the entire definition is memorized. An example is *res ipsa*, "negligence shortcut" and "rebuttable inference" – these four words seem to count the most. Another example is equal protection – no government discrimination against groups.

A related technique is to memorize certain words or phrases that "open the door" to the rest of the rule or principle. For example, for murder and manslaughter, the words might be "unlawful killing." For *res ipsa loquitur*, the words might be "rebuttable inference of negligence."

8. Technique #8: Memory Enhancers (acronyms and mnemonics)

Memory enhancers can be created by students from scratch or borrowed from others. These acronyms, mnemonics or other recall-enablers are highly recommended, given the overwhelming weight of the bar exam material. Lighten the load and have some fun doing it. For example, adverse possession is OCEAN for 20 – Open, Continuous, Exclusive, Adverse and Notorious for 20 years (at common law).

A popular way to enhance memory is mnemonics – words or acronyms that allow for easy recall. These words grease the memory process, especially under the time pressures of the bar exam.

9. *Technique #9: Doctrinal "Triggers"*

> Start with some facts – the bar
> examiners do.

Doctrinal triggers are facts that trigger legal issues. In a sense, these triggers are part of, and aid, critical reading. Instead of law then facts, the bar exam is facts then law – just like your law school exams. Why not study for the way you will be tested? It is useful to see economic laws passed by Congress as possibly triggering the commerce clause or the questions about a witness' truthfulness as triggering impeachment issues (unless the witness is a party, which may also trigger character evidence rules).

Legal rules can be located within larger doctrines and courses, such as provocation manslaughter. Provocation manslaughter, for example, resides within the doctrine of criminal homicide, which in turn lies within substantive criminal law. While this is useful information, it is just as helpful to determine what kind of fact patterns are associated with rules. One example is the commerce clause. Laws enacted by Congress that concern economic activities or movement of people or goods generally fall within the commerce clause power. The dormant commerce clause, on the other hand, concerns laws by states that discriminate against or unduly burden interstate commerce, so look for state laws that concern transportation or the sale or purchase of goods or services.

IX. CRITICAL WRITING TECHNIQUES

Chapter Points:
(1) Ditch IRAC – It's Too Vague and Manipulable.
(2) Go "Elemental" – Focus On Elements – Especially
 Pivotal Ones.
(3) Practice Regularly to Create Good Habits.
(4) Use Protocols for Writing.

A. CRITICAL WRITING TECHNIQUES

A lot of times, you may find yourself forsaking writing practice for two different reasons – you think you can get by without it, and let's face it, sometimes it seems tough and boring. Yet, writing for the bar examination is different than law school. In part because of the difference, it is also challenging.

> *In law school, a "note dump" on an exam often was received kindly, enhancing the perceived content –*
> *knowledge learned in the course. On the bar exam, a streamlined, focused answer is generally preferred.*

Practicing your writing could make all the difference in test scores. Here are some suggestions on how to practice.

Taking on a Role

If the examiner asks students to represent a particular party, they should write from that perspective. Students should not translate the questions to write their own particular answers. Further, essay answer choices are predictive. That means that students are predicting what the likely outcome is. Therefore, you've got to get used to writing with words such as "likely," "probably," "could be," and so on. If you try to predict a definitive conclusion, chances are you'll miss the whole point of writing the essay, which is to use the facts and the law to predict the best and most (or least) likely outcome.

Frame Your Art

Essay writing should be created like a piece of art – a frame should be around art and contain it in an orderly fashion. Thus, students should focus on how they are going to frame the very beginning and ending of their responses even before they start writing. To frame a question, it is extremely important to understand exactly what the question is asking. Too often, students start answering their own questions, rather than the particular call of the question asked by the examiner. This is very common and it's something you need to check yourself on. Remember, answer the questions the examiners are asking you, not the question you want to turn it into. Thus, if examiners ask students to write a memorandum, it should be in that form. If the examiners ask you to represent a particular party, then write from that perspective. Whatever you do, translate the questions to write your own preferred answers. If the question wants to know about the Free Exercise Clause, and the *Smith v. Oregon* test applies, don't think you can rack up some additional points by replacing it with the *Lemon v. Kurtzman* test used for the Establishment Clause. Just because both of these tests involve religion under the First Amendment does not mean that they are closely related enough to get points on a particular question or issue.

1. Technique #1: Identifying and Emphasizing Real Issues

The issue in an essay usually involves one or more rules. The *real* issue often involves only a portion of a rule, even a single element. For example, if the issue is negligence, the real issue is often duty, breach, causation OR damages – but not all four. This technique is a matter of emphasis – can the student focus the response on the "real issue" while giving a quick once over to the other elements? That is what *real issue* identification is about.

As noted above, identifying legal issues is a skill unto itself, but it is a skill students do not often isolate and practice. One reason issue identification ought to be practiced is that students answering essay questions often do not answer the precise question asked – and thus leave behind many of the points the question offers. Instead, students must learn to identify the precise issue. This means describing not just the general course area of the question – say property – and not just the entire legal rule or principle – say easements – but precisely which element or component is really disputed.

2. Technique #2: Mind the "Big Picture" and the Details

A big problem in writing for the bar exam is there is no "professor" you can use to help you orient yourself in writing your essays. Remember how you learned to take the professor and not the course in isolation? There are also many subjects that could be tested. So you must keep the "big picture" in mind – what are the subject areas that are being tested? Make sure you get the issues – and don't make any wrong turns at intersections. This is the "big picture." Then, watch the details – apply the pertinent rules carefully, without being conclusory. Both skills are needed for the bar exam.

Many test-takers lose sight of one or the other skill along the way. To elaborate, the "big picture" means the overall frameworks for each of the substantive courses (Constitutional Law: Powers v. Limits) and test-taking techniques, structures, for taking multiple choice questions and writing essays. The "details," on the other hand, are the elements of the rules (Murder: (1) The unlawful (2) killing of another human being (3) with malice) and, more importantly, the exceptions to those rules as well. For example, it is helpful to know that the Privileges and Immunities Clause of Article IV Section 2 is a limit on state discrimination against non-residents, but it is just as useful to know that the clause does not apply to non-fundamental discrimination against non-residents such as recreation. Knowing the details precisely – and being able to recall the knowledge quickly – is extremely important.

B. PRACTICE, PRACTICE, PRACTICE

A lot of people really drop the ball when it comes to doing multiple choice questions or essay writing. Very few law students practice legal writing for the fun of it. Let's face it, there are other things you could be doing, such as watching a movie or surfing the Northshore of the Hawaiian coast.

For that matter, fewer students practice it, even when their careers are on the line - namely, when they are studying for the bar exam. It is ironic that with all of the money and effort expended in preparing for the bar exam, most test-takers write their first full-length essay under time pressure at the actual exam itself. Even professional athletes have "spring training" or "exhibition" games in which to prepare for the actual contests.

It is somewhat understandable that students do not regularly practice their writing during bar preparations. In law school, exam preparation did not routinely include essay writing under time pressure, but rather centered on notes, outlines and oral interaction. For the bar exam, the focus often is displaced - on coverage and the mass of raw material.

C. DITCH IRAC ("CRAC" is Better)

> <u>Go Elemental</u>: Generally state the precise elements of a cause of action or defense.

IRAC allows students to feel like they are following a protocol when the map is not really well-defined. It is so loose and malleable there are few limits – it is a lot like the speed limit when no police are around. Without enforcement, it is illusory.

During your bar course and all throughout law school, others probably preached the virtues of using IRAC when writing your exam essays. Let's quickly review this silly acronym. You're supposed to spot the issue and then list it, address the rules of that issue, analyze (whatever that really means) and then write a conclusion. Issue, Rule, Analysis, Conclusion. What's wrong with this picture? Well, for starters, IRAC is so flexible that bar-takers never really use it the way it's intended to be used. IRAC is used to fit whatever you want to write in your essay, so people who are practicing writing never really end up writing it the same way on the bar exam. Why? Because they often practice it in a shorthand version to save time and energy like it's a mere note-taking exercise as opposed to actually writing a full-length answer for the bar examiners. When you turn in your bar exam essays, you need to have the framework down on how you are actually going to answer a question in full and how the bar examiners are going to grade it. Many jurisdictions want an answer and some want it up front. This yields "CRAC" – Conclusion, Rule, Application, Conclusion.

If the question is about an equitable servitude in Property, for example, the bar examiners don't merely want to see that an equitable servitude is a restriction on the use of land that counts as an interest in land, enforceable in equity. The examiners want to see the precise elements. An equitable servitude requires:

(1) A covenant between the landowners,
(2) with an intention to bind the restriction to the land itself and not a person.
    If so, the servitude might run with the land if

(3) a transferee takes with the actual or constructive notice of the servitude and

(4) the covenant touches and concerns the land.

If you leave any of those elements out, you're not really analyzing the problem correctly. [Now, you may be wondering about privity of estate. It is not required when equitable relief is sought. Privity of estate (POE) means that there is a mutual interest in land between two parties. A landlord and tenant have POE and a tenant and sub-tenant might have POE (depending on whether the entire interest has transferred). In actions at law, seeking damages, privity of estate is required.]

ESSAY EXAMPLE

<u>Hypothetical</u>: Jennifer found her boyfriend Brad in bed kissing the mail woman, Angelina. In a psychotic rage, she hit Brad in the head with a hammer. He died nine months later from his wounds.

<u>Conclusion</u>: "It appears that Jennifer murdered Brad.
<u>Elements</u>: Murder is the:

(1) Unlawful (2) Killing of another human being (3) With malice.

To commit murder with malice is to commit it:

(1) Purposely, (2) Knowingly or (3) With Gross Recklessness. [Now that there are at least two main elements, the act of killing another and the mental state of malice, the application of each element in separate paragraphs can occur.] However, since Jennifer walked in on Brad with Angelina, Jennifer was probably upset. Therefore, it may have been voluntary manslaughter, specifically provocation manslaughter. After the murder

analysis concludes, the provocation manslaughter analysis can begin. Provocation manslaughter is an:

(1) Intentional killing of another
(2) Mitigated by adequate (actual and reasonable) provocation in the "heat of passion"
(3) Without actual or reasonable time to cool off.

Okay, you see what we did there? We're not saying it's conclusively murder or voluntary manslaughter while leaving the other one out. We're starting out with the larger crime of murder (a general strategy in criminal law – go large first), since the fact pattern, some of which we're leaving up to your imagination, appears to be about murder. However, it's a close call, so we're going to throw in voluntary manslaughter as well. Just so you know, kissing might be adequate provocation to be in the heat of passion, although kissing is likely not as provocative as other acts. Nonetheless, we're throwing it in there just to cover our bases!

There may be a defense involved here because Jennifer acted in "a psychotic rage." Maybe Jennifer wants to use the affirmative defense of insanity. This defense is waivable and need not be asserted (as compared to competency, which cannot be waived). A major common law test for insanity is the M'Naghten Test. Under the M'Naghten Test, defendants are relieved of criminal liability upon proof that at the time they committed the crime, they were suffering from a severe mental disease or defect which caused them not to know the nature of the act they were committing or not to be able to distinguish right from wrong. The "Irresistible Impulse Test," which acquits defendants who have a mental disease or defect that kept them from controlling their conduct, has been adopted by a minority of jurisdictions. The Durham Test, which holds that a defendant is not criminally liable if his or her unlawful act was the product of mental disease or defect, has been widely eliminated. Don't use this test.

However, if you're in a state like New York or California that follows the Model Penal Code, you won't want to forget about the "Substantial Capacity Test," which dictates that people are not guilty of a crime if, at the time they committed the crime, they lacked substantial capacity to appreciate the wrongfulness of their act or the requirements of the law. What's a good essay writer to do? A good essay writer who is not in a Model Penal Code state will start out with the majority rule. Remember, the key is writing about everything that could apply. That doesn't mean you write about the possibility of Double Jeopardy applying after Jennifer gets convicted and re-tried if the conviction is tossed on appeal. It just means that if there's a rule or issue that applies, we want you to use "whole rule analysis." Remember, the bar examiners wrote these questions with a particular framework in mind and they're hungering for essays that reflect right back to them those frameworks and protocols, just like a mirror.

D. BOX IT UP

As we've said before, every time you face a problem, you must state the entire rule, especially its entire set of elements. When appropriate, make a brief recitation of what an element means and then dive into the analysis. When people buy a new computer program, too often they pop the disc in their computer without actually reading the instructions. You should pretend that your essay is much like a set of instructions.

You're taking the reader through a step-by-step process on whatever topic you're covering. For instance, when answering a question about breach of contract, you should first address whether a valid contract even exists. Expert responses should cover the basic steps and highlight the most basic aspect of whatever the problem is. It's about highlighting, emphasis, and, most importantly, communication. You're an expert now that you've graduated from law school, and you need to write these explanations as if they're for a prospective client who knows nothing about the law. Box it up - keep it together, clean and tight. Don't go wandering but explain yourself fully on the relevant issues and elements.

Lastly, don't make up your own issue or what you think is interesting. Let's say the question asks about the creation of an easement, which could occur by:

(1) Implication (necessity or conveyance) an
(2) Express grant (in favor of conveyee) or reservation (in favor of conveyor),
(3) Prescription (adverse possession),
(4) Estoppel or
(5) Eminent domain.

If these possibilities could apply, then include the entire list. If not, include only what could apply. If you've forgotten about the ways to create easements, don't start rambling instead about how an "appurtenant easement" is attached to another piece of land that benefits the owner of that land as opposed to an "easement in gross" that only requires one piece of land where the holder is not benefited - unless the question asks for that.

It may be appropriate to write about how an easement is extinguished, but only if it is relevant. If you've got the time, consider mentioning that easements can be extinguished by:

(1) An express writing,
(2) Merger (when the dominant and servient tenement come under the ownership of the same person),
(3) Condemnation of the servient estate,
(4) Abandonment evidenced by clear intent,
(5) The destruction of the servient tenement,
(6) Prescription or
(7) Estoppel.

Our message is clear. Don't do an "information dump" and try to distract the bar examiners with what you know if you can't answer the question the way it's asked. Focus your energies elsewhere with the time you have or write about whatever issues are rationally related (to borrow a phrase from Constitutional Law) to the question. You might have been taught you can't lose points in law school for writing things that are inaccurate. Technically, on the bar exam you probably won't lose points either. But here's the trick. If you stray, it will disrupt your form and substance. Remember - you're getting points for what you write and how you write it. If you write about issues that have no bearing on the question, you are distracting yourself. You also may frustrate a bar grader and your essay may get fewer points than it deserves.

Too many students are concerned with getting the absolute right answer and end up throwing answers all over the place. Like drawers for shirts, socks and your rugby uniform, everything should be specific and separated. A paragraph that focuses on a rule should stay focused on the rule and not start delving into the facts.

E. USE ANCHOR AND TRIGGER WORDS

Anchors Away

Anchor words help you clue in to what a general area involves. Too many students try to remember the entire paragraph or paragraphs of a rule and really end up learning none of it. For instance, instead of "runs with the land" you can simply remember "runs." This way, you can remember to add "with the land" later. Or, if while examining a Privileges and Immunities question and the issue involves a law disfavoring non-state residents, you can remember just "discrimination non-state" because you will remember residents later. For malice, just remember "PKR," instead of "purposely, knowingly, and recklessly." Instead of trying to create three separate sentences of what it means, use an acronym.

In addition to the actual words of legal significance, there are words that help frame your answer that, in turn, help you recall the rule. We call these words trigger words. For instance, in Constitutional Law, we use trigger words to distinguish the Commerce Clause, Privileges and Immunities and Equal Protection. Here are some examples.

ANCHOR AND TRIGGER WORDS

Constitutional Law:

1. Dormant Commerce Clause: (Triggers) State limit on discrimination against favoring own commerce as burdening commerce.
    (Anchors) (a) No Discrimination (b) Against (c) Interstate Commerce

2. Privileges and Immunities Clause: (Triggers) State limit on discrimination against non-residents in the state.
    (Anchors) (a) Discrimination (b) Against (c) Non-State Residents

3. Equal Protection: (Triggers) government (State or Federal) limit on bad discrimination.
    (Anchors) (a) No Discrimination (b) Against (c) Groups

4. Procedural Due Process: (Triggers) limit on government (State or Federal) often deprivation of jobs or benefits.
    (Anchors) (a) Government deprivation of life, liberty or property and then (b) balancing test, notice and/or hearing.

Property:

1. Affirmative Easements: (Triggers) Legal right to use another's property.
    (Anchors) (a) Right to use another's land (b) Irrevocable (c) Writing

2. Easements Not Requiring Writing: (Triggers) Implied by law.
   (Anchors) (a) Prescriptive (b) Necessity (c) Implied by prior use

3. Rule Against Perpetuities: (Triggers) Limit on transfer of land to third party.
   (Anchors) (a) Limit (b) On Transfer of Real Property to (c) Third Party (Grantee).

4. Real Covenant: (Triggers) Limit on use of own land
   (Anchors) (a) Limit (b) Use of own real property (c) Agreement (d) Might run with land

5. License: (Triggers) Legal right to temporarily use another's property.
   (Anchors) (a) Right to use another's property (b) Revocable (c) (Generally) Oral

Evidence:

1. Refreshing Recollection: (Triggers) Testifying witness needs help remembering facts.
   (Anchors) (a) Witness forgets (b) Any evidence spurs memory and (c) witness remembers

2. Best Evidence Rule: (Triggers) Writing contents are legally important to case.
   (Anchors) (a) If Proving Contents (b) Need original or "sweet 'n low" substitute

   Anchor and trigger words help the student reach the best answer. For instance, so why is the best evidence rule often the wrong answer? It is because the only time the best evidence rule is the correct response is when a party is proving the contents of a writing. It usually deals with a deed, will or contract of some kind. Don't ever fall for the answer in an evidence question where they won't admit a recording, piece of evidence or someone's testimony because it's not the best evidence unless there is an actual writing (including recordings, x0rays and the like)and the contents are at issue in the case. An example would be those mysterious military records that demonstrated accusations against President Bush of not showing up for service when he was in the Texas Air Force National Guard. Dan Rather reported the story, but the contents of the documents came into question later because the typeface seemed too new to date back to the typewriters that were in existence during the Vietnam War. If there was ever a civil suit concerning those documents, the trier of fact may require the original documents that Dan Rather relied on since the documents themselves were in issue.

X. <u>THE APPROACH TO GAME DAY</u>

Chapter Points
(1) Don't Panic.
(2) Change Your Studying Process to Reviewing.
(3) Start by Working Backwards.

A. THREE WEEKS TO GO

1. Schedule

Okay, here's a basic schedule for you to keep in mind for the last three weeks. Up until now, you should have done several hundred, if not a thousand or more, multistate questions. No, we didn't say "several hundred thousand questions" – pay attention! And, stop freaking out. We said *either* several hundred, if not a thousand questions, so chill out. Really, cool your jets and pipe down. That's the whole point of this chapter. We're here to put you at ease and remind you to be cool. Is it working so far?

Write Your Response Here: _____

If your answer was yes, we commend you.
If your answer was no, well, whatever; keep your opinions to yourself from now on, okay? And since you need to cool off, go treat yourself to a pint of Ben & Jerry's ice cream.

Feel better? Well, you should. We're doing the best we can and you've got to get more positive. Of course you're probably getting nervous. But, so what? You've got nothing to be nervous about if you're on schedule, and that's what's important. Of course you will have done hundreds of questions by now and you've either attended classes or taken a home study course. You're ready for lift off. We're just going to give you a few tips on how to keep those engines cool until it's time.

131

Here's what you want to start working on. It is step #1. Stick to a schedule. For example, you want to start to review all the basic course frameworks and know how to use them. Remember the basic course frameworks. If you get to a Torts question, you should automatically apply the framework and ask yourself, *"Which subject area am I in?"*

2. Nerves

Don't pretend you're not nervous. We know you are, so just accept it. Don't try to avoid feeling nervous. Instead, simply accept that it's okay to be nervous. Once you've accepted it, channel that nervous energy properly by attacking your course work and help transform it into confidence. One of the most important things to do during this exam is not to doubt your abilities. This is crucial.

a. Cool as Ice

> This test is your Olympic marathon; pace yourself so you are peaking at race-time.

It is extremely common, especially after taking those bar review courses that hype you up to be on the lookout for trick questions, to doubt yourself when you instinctively see the right answer. You may see a "gimme" question that poses a simple question and gives you a clear set of three wrong answers. However, instead of picking the right answer when you see it, you may pick an alternative answer because you've never seen it before or it sounds like it could be right. Look, you've pretty much covered the gamut. If you see something you don't recognize, chances are it's a red herring and you need to steer clear of it.

It's very, very common for bar-takers to see an answer they know is right in their heart but avoid choosing it. It can be that one answer that leaves you one point shy of passing. Take it from us, it's happened. We're not suggesting that you don't methodically analyze questions and feel certain that you are picking the right answer. You should always be cautious and cool when analyzing questions. However, if you feel strongly that an answer is right, go for it. Remember that character from *West Side Story* named Ice with those cool blue eyes? He was the one who took over the leadership of the Jets after their original leader Riff was killed by their rivals in a secret rumble by the waterfront. After the rumble was over and the cops were looking to round everyone up, Ice had some wisdom that helped him prevail as the Jets' new leader. "If you wanna make it in this lousy world, ya gotta play it cool." Well, he was right. Play it cool - cool as our friend Ice. You'll stay out of trouble and get home free and clear.

b. Avoid Quicksand

Another important piece of advice is not to obsess over a question. If you can't find the answer, if you're just not seeing it and after two minutes go by you just can't grasp it, let it go. It's not as if another seven minutes of dwelling on it will help you. Remember, for every minute you spend on one question you can't answer, you're deducting time from other questions you have the capacity to answer because they're within the scope of what you studied and retained. And now that the bar examiners on the multistate are throwing in practice questions to be "pretested," there is absolutely no reason to linger. Besides, there are always a group of exceedingly hard questions that are thrown on the bar exam that even the best bar-takers can't figure out. Consider these questions "quicksand." We believe these questions are systematically designed to slow you down and get you stuck. The longer you obsess over these questions, the more you will sink lower and lower both in the sense of time lost and in terms of your confidence. After spending a good six minutes on one question and still realize you could not confidently figure it out, you will be blown away and unsure of yourself. This is the worst possible thing that can happen to you during an exam (short of incorrectly marking your answers on the answer sheet). When you see a question that is just completely perplexing you, do yourself a favor. Take your best shot and move on. It will empower you. Remind yourself, *you're* in control of this exam, not the bar examiners.

3. Natural as Granola

Okay, you're almost home free. You've been studying and you're getting stressed out. You've got to take it down a notch. Keep the momentum going, but remember that it may not kill you to take a few hours off or maybe even a day. On the subject of granola, make sure you're eating well. Remember, you are what you eat. We mean that if you're eating badly, you won't be thinking clearly. Get some iron into your blood. If necessary, cook a steak at home and put on a good movie with your Golden Retriever.

Actually, when we say that you need to be "natural as granola" we mean that it's okay for you to accept that you are going to get nervous about this exam. You're probably already nervous. Okay, you're nervous; but so what? Just say it's okay. Realize you're going to get nervous and realize how much you've done. This is no different than riding a bike; it's automatic and reflexive. After all, you've been studying your tail off. You know more than you ever have. Act like an expert and boost your confidence. Explain some criminal law scenarios to non-law student friends of yours who will stare at you in awe as you explain the most recent "Law & Order" episode they just watched. You're the expert. Just relax and stay the course.

4. Stay the Course

> Knowledge only matters if you can move it from your outline to your brain.

Knowledge is only helpful if you can say it quickly and succinctly at "Mach-3 speed." It's not enough to have it in your outline. It has to be readily accessible in your brain. Remember, you need to start practicing jumping from course to course and rule to rule because that's exactly how it is on the bar. Write every single day. Write rules and elements. If you're not writing it then you're not thinking it. Writing the rules and elements helps you get rid of the fuzziness. You've got to go for clarity. Don't ditch an entire subject to save for "later," whenever that will be. When you practice a subject, make sure you master – not just study, but master – at least one rule in a subject during each study session.

> Don't become a rules skimmer; still
> master one rule at a time.

Here's another thought. With only three weeks to go, you should start simulating exam conditions. Feel what it's like and start acting like the bar is tomorrow. Take note of how much time it takes for you to get up and fall asleep. Also take heed of when you eat and what kind of physical impact certain foods have on you around lunchtime. If a turkey sandwich makes you tired, avoid that on exam day. If a cheeseburger makes you sick, ditch that too. Make sure you start sleeping on a schedule that parallels the same schedule for exam week. Don't suddenly switch your schedules or routines. Determine what works for you and make a routine practice of it for the next weeks and then stick with it.

5. Do You Feel Lucky?

Good. We don't like "Lady Luck," but if you're feeling lucky, it probably means you're feeling confident. Just don't get over-confident and start slacking. If you're not feeling lucky, then use that energy to channel it into some solid studying to boost your morale. If you need a break, however, even if you just bombed out on a set of Property questions, take a break. It doesn't help to push yourself so hard you're not thinking clearly. Luck is usually a veil for confidence, fear or both. Try to feel confident, fearless while keeping your tasks in perspective.

6. Take a Walk

No, really, just take a walk. Get some fresh air. Go out for a bike ride or something and get some physical activity again. You've probably been sitting down for like 8-10 hours per day, and that's not good for you. You've got to release some endorphins because it will help your mind work again. (A study found that physical exercise gets the brain pumping as well.) In fact, if your back is hurting, you may want to go get a massage and get those knots out before you're stuck in the exam room for 16 hours over a two day period. If you're in pain now, try to address this problem at least a week before the exam.

7. I Have Studied and I Have Learned

Like we said earlier, you are the bar exam expert now. Maybe you don't know everything you could know; heck, maybe you only learned 50% of what you need to know. Whatever you did this time around, you did the best you could at this point and once you hit the end point, you need to really know in your heart that you've learned more than you ever have and that you have a decent chance of passing this exam. You studied Contracts, and you know that a "Requirements/Outputs Contract" requires:

a. Vocabulary, saying "All I require" or "all I can produce" and not "all I desire," or "all I want."
b. You also know that if a requirements/outputs contracts does have the incorrect language as the result of either a typing or secretarial error, the court will reform the

contract so that it reflects the actual intent of the parties and render it valid.

You see? You knew that. If you didn't know it, well you know it now, so stop worrying. We mentioned this little nugget because a requirements contracts question is seemingly on almost every MBE and the question either involves the particular language used, as discussed before, or a reformation issue arising due to a clerical error. You just went up one point. You have studied and learned.

8. Toxic People

Get that radioactive-proof suit off and remove those goggles. We're not suggesting people are actually toxic or radioactive. What we mean is that there are people out there who haven't studied as hard as you have and they're going to be a detriment to you. They're going to be freaking out and if you listen to them panicking and re-analyzing rules you already have mastered, they're going to make you question your own confidence and freak you out, too. This is particularly true when you get to your hotel in the days before the exam.

Here's a familiar scenario for you to expect. Okay, it's the day before the exam and you've just pulled up to your hotel (preferably a Marriott, but maybe you can only afford a Holiday Inn – whatever, as long as it's clean and close to the exam site, we're good to go). You get out of your car and check in. You notice a barrage of law students walking around in pairs and triplets. You'll see some people in the hotel bar drinking. These might be takers who, for whatever reason, seem to think that they can operate better on alcohol. We don't recommend this path, especially since most of you reading this book haven't taken the bar yet, so stay away from the bar.

You get into the elevator, and ah, there he is. You know, that guy. He's that guy that wasn't really very popular and wants to impress others in the elevator so he starts telling his friend about the specific, detailed differences involving conspiracy analyses under common law as opposed to the Model Penal Code. He's talking kind of loud to make sure that everyone can hear him, and he's kind of acting half cool, yet half paranoid and shooting his mouth off in every direction. Ironically, half of what he's saying is probably inaccurate.

Don't engage or try to correct this guy. Make sure to stay away from him and anyone else carrying a bar exam review book. Go to your room and relax. If you want to order room service or get a bite with a familiar face, go for it. Just don't start debating complex rules with people you don't know. They probably don't know what they're talking about and they're just going to get you hyped up and stressed out. Who needs it?

Just stay focused and play it cool so avoid toxic people – relatives included – especially with one week to go.

B. ONE WEEK TO GO

The week before the exam is a time when you should "stay the course" personally and professionally. This is not the time to start a diet, relationship or hobby or end one. It is also not the time to dramatically change study habits. Those who cram are going to want to start a "24/7" scorched earth policy of learning everything at all hours, but remember, this exam is just like a big athletic contest and you want to stick to your carefully constructed training regime. As noted in the toxic people section above, this is the time you put out the "do not disturb" sign – even for relatives and close friends. If they just don't get it, then they are not acting in your best interest. Other bar-takers may turn into toxic, needy people the week before the exam as well, so beware.

Because this is just like preparing for a big athletic event, you must take care of your body and mind. This means eating well, getting some sleep and working on self-confidence. If this means listening to your favorite music and watching an episode of your favorite comedy show, go for it. A little laughter and inspirational music can go a long way.

1. Keep Staying the Course – Confirm and Sail

Whatever it is you've been doing the past couple of weeks, keep it up. By now, you've conditioned yourself how to study, and the worst thing you can do is change gears to another supplement or set of outlines. Just stick with what you know, confirm your knowledge and reinstall your confidence in the material.

We've said it before and we'll say it again, but you can't learn every last bit of the material that exists for the bar exam. It's impossible. Therefore, you need to avoid traps that take you into quicksand. Don't start learning new exceptions the day before the exam. It takes time to learn something and you may confuse yourself. What appears to be a rule may actually be an exception, and what appears to be a valid exception may be a minority rule that is no longer accepted as the general rule. You're much better off just solidifying what you already know and making sure you can name the rule, elements and exceptions on the tip of your tongue.

2. Focus

It isn't uncommon to start running out of fuel about a week before the exam. It's healthy to take solid breaks to energize yourself, but whatever you do, don't start working on alternative projects around the house or pick up a novel to relax. You need to keep your mind focused on bar material.

I know it sounds hard to imagine, but it isn't uncommon for people to escape their fear and frustration by channeling their physical or mental energy into these alternative projects when they get close to exam time. We've already discussed the fear factor and how it's natural and healthy to accept that fear, so don't worry about it. If you can find outlets to vent your frustration and clear your head, like taking a quick swim or working on your web site, go ahead. Just don't get wrapped up in anything. Your focus is critical.

Another common problem is relationships. It's very common at this point for your significant other or your friends to express their own frustration over the fact that you're "never around" and so dedicated to your studies. Tell your friends to take a rain check. They can vent all they want over a pizza and pitcher of root beer in a couple of weeks.

If you're encountering personal problems with someone you live with, you may have to actually go stay with someone else or bite the bullet and invest in a hotel room. Whatever problems you're encountering short of medical crises, stay focused on the bar exam. Don't let anything or anyone distract you. It's not worth it.

3. The Day Before the Exam

Resting the day before the exam to avoid burn-out is actually strategic bar preparation.

Like most law students, you're probably conditioned to study hard even the day before the exam. In fact, you may think it's wise to study right up to the last minute. With the bar exam, that's a serious mistake. This isn't a two or three hour exam. The test's duration is nearly eight hours, including your lunch break.

One of the most important factors in your performance is going to be your endurance. You need to remain focused and energized throughout the exam and this is difficult. Most students find themselves hitting a brick wall somewhere around question 140. For some reason, this appears to be the magic number. It may be typical amount of time has passed for the food you've digested to hit your bloodstream while having a neurological impact. The authors are not doctors, so don't take this as fact. It's just a guess, but the fact is that many people start to run low on "fuel" during the exam.

There are two ways to try and minimize this detrimental impact. First of all, try to eat a solid, but light lunch. We'll talk more about this later. For now, we want to preach the concept of resting to you. It's okay if you periodically want to breeze through an outline the day before the exam here and there. However, for the most part, you should do whatever you like to do as if it were mostly a day off. Try watching a movie or doing a little light window-shopping at the mall since it should be a Monday or Tuesday. Whatever you do, keep it low-key and try not to think about the exam.

4. The Night Before the Exam

> If you can't sleep the night before the exam, just lie there.

The night before the exam is the one time you may want to read a little material or study. Tuck yourself in and read something incredibly boring. Try reading an outline. It will serve as a little refresher but might bore you if you just read rule after rule. 401, 402, 403, 404, 405 ... You'll find yourself getting tired and sleepy and hopefully you'll drift off. If not, just lie there. Don't try to sneak in some extra studying instead of sleep. It will come back to haunt you.

Jeff Says:

The night before the Florida bar exam, my friend Dan and I arrived in Tampa International Airport and got a shuttle to the Marriott Hotel across the street. It was 9 p.m. by the time we settled into our room, and we turned out the lights by 9:30. Unfortunately, we weren't the least bit tired. The two of us were wide-awake all night long. Our adrenaline was racing so fast that we couldn't catch a wink. Instead of talking to one another to at least pass the time and get sleepy, we tried to fall asleep.

Nonetheless, we both knew the other person was awake and there was that occasional whisper from one person to the other: "Hey, are you still up?" and the proverbial answer – "No, genius . . . I'm sound asleep." It was a total disaster. We would have been much better off forcing ourselves to go for a light run or reading some rules-based material to get sleepy. Turning off the light wasn't enough to cut it. In this circumstance, I made sure to just accept my fate. I got up at 6 a.m. and ate as early as possible so that I could get it over with. After I ate, I got tired about an hour later from my breakfast and then rejuvenated. By the time 9 a.m. rolled around, I was ready to take the exam. I wasn't in the best state of mind, but I made the best circumstance of a bad situation. The lesson here is that you need to do whatever you can to fall asleep naturally. If you force it, you'll only stress yourself out and not fall asleep at all. If this happens, revert back to this backup plan. Get up early, eat breakfast to get it over with, take your restroom break before the exam, relax and energize yourself. At 9 a.m. you won't be as sleepy as many other people.

XI. <u>THE EXAM IS NOW - STRATEGIES AND TACTICS</u>

Chapter Points
(1) Relax.
(2) Make an early hotel reservation.
(3) Clothing – Not too warm, not too cold.

A. DISMANTLING PRESSURE

Congratulations, you've finally made it to the bar exam. It's time for you to give it your all and put this chapter of your life behind you. Make sure you have this positive outlook. This is an opportunity for you to move forward in life. Every minute that passes is one step closer to finishing this exam. There are some people who look at the clock as a ticking time bomb, dreading every moment that they get closer to exam time. Instead, we suggest the alternative perspective. You should realize that every minute you get closer to the exam, the closer you are to being finished with it. As we said in earlier chapters, this day is going to go more quickly than any other day of your life. You will get tired and frustrated, but you will also feel exhilarated.

It's very simple. You've done hundreds, if not thousands, of practice questions by now. Now you're going to have a chance to see what it's like to apply that knowledge to the real thing. It may sound improbable, but this experience may actually be fun for you. Just kick back and enjoy the challenge. In a few hours you'll be driving or flying home and feeling a terrific sense of accomplishment.

B. CLOTHING

Needless to say, this is not a day you need to sport your finest pair of Cole Haan shoes or your best Polo shirt. There are a few places, like Virginia, that have a conservative dress code, but absent this unusual rule, you should focus on one element only – comfort!

The most common bar exam outfit is a pair of sweats or jeans with a t-shirt and sweater. Wear your most comfortable pair of shoes and take it easy. Like we said before, you're going to be very focused. You probably wouldn't notice it if Angelina Jolie or Brad Pitt were sitting beside you. This isn't a day to impress anyone or flirt, so regardless of who's going to be there (an old flame from law school or college), just forget about that. You can send a bouquet of flowers later.

Whatever you do, don't wear shorts or clothing so heavy that you lose control over your own body temperature should the examiners turn up the air conditioning or heat. You need to stay in control of your own comfortability and that's why we recommend blue jeans or khaki's with a soft sweatshirt, preferably with a zipper, for additional climate control.

C. FOOD

We promised to get into food in the previous chapter, so we're going to keep our word. The night before the exam, eat something that gives you some strength but nothing that you know can make you feel sick. You know your own body, so play it smart. If something makes you have an allergy attack or makes you feel queasy, avoid it.

What's more important is what you eat the following day when you're actually taking the exam. Eat a solid breakfast that will get your mind working, but don't eat so much it makes you sleepy. If a little coffee will wake you up, that is fine, just don't drink so much that it causes frequent restroom visits. Remember that coffee is a diuretic. The earlier you eat, the more time your body will have to process it, and hopefully whatever impact it has on you (sleepiness or digestion) will occur prior to exam time.

The most important meal of your life will probably be lunchtime, particularly when you take the multistate section. Once again, avoid heavy foods that will make you sleepy. Avoid turkey because it contains tryptophan, which makes you sleepy. Milk contains lactose and that also makes you sleepy. Your best bet, believe it or not, is a good bowl of soup and some crackers. Don't drink too much water, to avoid frequent restroom breaks. If you find yourself having to take a restroom break, utilize the time wisely. If you stumble across a difficult question, and you're torn between two answers, take a walk to the restroom and think about it. You'll be surprised. Taking a moment away from the exam booklet may even clear your head a little.

D. HOUSING

This is a critical aspect of the bar exam experience. We strongly advise you to make reservations several months or even a year in advance. The city that is hosting the bar exam is most likely going to be booked solid by the time you arrive.

You're better off staying at a hotel as close to the bar exam site as possible. The best case scenario is staying somewhere within walking distance. This will help you to avoid unnecessary traffic, rushing and complications in the morning. There's another issue. You aren't staying in your hotel after the second test day, which means that you have to check out that morning. Therefore, you either need to take your luggage with you to the exam, leave it in the trunk of your car in a paid parking garage or leave it with the concierge at your hotel and return to it later on. You're much better off simply leaving it with the concierge at a hotel across the street from the exam site, walking back and making for a quick getaway when it's over.

Another critical issue is making sure that you either have your own room or at least your own bed, since your friend's sleeping habits can become disruptive.

Barbara and Jenna:

Barbara and Jenna reserved a hotel room months in advance in Austin to take the Texas bar exam. They didn't ask about the bed accommodations, so they ended up with a King size bed. They tried to switch to a room that had two double beds, but the front desk clerk told them that the hotel was now completely booked. All night long, the two of them were shifting around keeping one another awake. A couple of times they kicked one another. At one point, Jenna accidentally kicked Barbara off the bed. At dawn, the two were half awake from a rough night and annoyed with one another and exhausted.

The lesson here is simple. Make your hotel reservations in advance as long before the exam as possible. If you're sharing a room to save money or to keep an ally close to you, make sure you have two double beds. If you're a non-smoker, make sure the room is non-smoking. You don't need any respiratory problems during the night.

Last but not least, ask the front desk for a wake up call. If you live locally or elect to stay with a friend, ask someone dependable to call you at the appropriate time in addition to setting an alarm. The exam generally starts at 9 a.m., and the examiners usually request that you're there an hour beforehand, so you shouldn't get up much later than 7 a.m. You may even want to get up earlier as we discussed in previous sections.

E. THE EXAM ITSELF - TIME, TOOLS, TEMPER-AMENT, READING AND FRAMEWORKS

You wake up in your room and dim light is passing through the curtains. Your first thought is probably, "Whoa." That's right. Today is the day. After several weeks of around-the-clock studying, you're on your way. You're armed with your I.D. and your bar examination ticket – maybe a set of pencils, depending on whether the examiners will supply you with some

146

or not. Even if they have, it doesn't hurt to have your own sharpened set. It will give you more ability to keep using sharp pencils instead of being stuck with a couple of dull ones.

Take a hot shower and relax for a little while. Have breakfast, maybe even turn on the news and watch a morning show. Don't start panicking and studying. Just take it easy and play it cool, like our friend, Ice. You're going to be just fine. If anything, you should feel a bit of excitement. Before you leave, make sure of the following - You have your I.D., your exam ticket, both socks on your feet (unless you opted for flip flops in Florida or California) and you are leaving your cell phone behind. Let us reiterate this last point. Do not, under any circumstances, take your cell phone into the testing site. It's against the rules and if your phone rings during the exam, you'll have the very special privilege of taking the exam over six months from now because likely you'll be disqualified.

When you finally leave your hotel room, you're going to step into an elevator full of other bar-takers. There will most likely be a wave of silence, not to mention the smell of fear. Don't sweat it. Remember, most law students are a type "A" personality and they're worried about perfection. You, on the other hand, have read this book and know the secret to the bar exam. You only need to pass – and you're going to pass.

After you get to the test site, there are going to be a series of tables where you check in according to your last name. If you have a laptop computer for an essay test, you're better off putting it in a disposable bag so you don't have to check a backpack or laptop bag since most tests centers won't allow them inside. If you stayed in a hotel, use a disposable, plastic laundry bag and then throw it away inside. If you live in a place where the weather is snowy or rainy, this option may not be available depending on the morning weather conditions.

Once you get checked in, in some jurisdictions you'll exchange your bar examination ticket for a badge that has your passport-size photo on it. It should look familiar because it's the one you mailed in a few months ago when you sent in your exam application. Chances are you were asked to show up at least an hour before the test actually starts, so you may find yourself waiting around for a while with nothing to do. Talk to your friends if it makes you feel comfortable, but try to avoid enhancing one another's fears.

Once the test doors open, you'll be ushered into a big room with lots of fold out tables and chairs. You will be assigned to your seat by an identification number on your badge, and there will be signs directing you to the proper area. There may also be large digital clocks that count down from 3 hours since the exam is in 3-hour increments.

You'll arrive at your desk and most likely will be sitting beside someone you've never met before. Introduce yourself if you want and find something to talk about. (Or be unsociable – that is perfectly acceptable here. The goal is to pass the bar exam, not make a new friend.) As hard as you try to talk about something else, you'll most likely both discuss how unfamiliar the strange test conditions are. Almost everyone taking the exam has the same conversation. The repeat takers or lawyers moving in state who have already taken the bar will be a bit less chatty. They know the drill. At the front of the room, there will be an announcer who will be talking in a very monotone voice, telling you not to open your test booklet and where the restrooms are. It's extremely annoying and often makes people more nervous.

Whatever you do, make sure you don't open your test booklet until they say to do so. In fact, don't even touch it. Just leave that booklet alone. You can sit and close your eyes. Or another way to pass the time and make valuable use of it is to escape the testing room in the restroom. That's right. Just walk into the restroom, check into a private stall and take a deep breath. It will help you avoid all the nerve-racked conditions on the outside. If you're so inclined, you can make valuable use of this situation by actually going to the bathroom. Remember, you only have a minute and 48 seconds per question once the test begins, so you're better off taking care of whatever business you can before the test starts.

The Exam is Now -- Strategies and Tactics

At a certain time, the announcer will tell you to remove your answer sheet from your booklet without opening it. Obey these instructions and fill out the bubble answer sheet (name, address, state) as you are directed. Then, when they tell you that "you may begin," tear that booklet open and go to town.

Here's our simple advice. Treat this test seriously, but just sail through it as you did with your practice questions. If you did relatively well on those, you'll probably do well on these, even if they look a bit different. Remember, this is a bar exam – not a medical exam. The worst-case scenario is not that you're going to die. You're just going to have to take it over. It's really not the end of the world. Your professors, bar instructors, fellow students and the test center conditions enhance the paranoia of how important this test is, but put it in perspective.

As you are analyzing a question, remember the frameworks. Look at the answers and the call of the question. Determine what subject area of law you're in and then read the question carefully. Be conscious of how you are dancing through each problem. Work assertively and energetically and take one last look at your answer and the fact pattern before moving on if time permits to make sure you didn't miss a word that changes the legal analysis. Don't re-analyze the whole fact pattern. You're merely looking for a word or two that changes the legal outcome of the answer. Then, move on.

XII. <u>POST-MORTEMS</u>

Chapter Points
(1) Have No Regrets.

A. AFTER A QUESTION

Once you've finished a question, be sure of your answer before marking it. The reason for this is simple. Erasing answers on these particular scantron sheets can be tricky. You never know when the scantron machine is going to sense lead remnants from the erased answer and then detect two answers on one question. If this occurs, it will automatically mark the answer as wrong. We're not saying not to erase answers, but you should try to avoid it whenever possible.

After you've answered a question, you may feel a sense of doubt. Unless you have a specific reason for this, you should immediately move on to the next question with confidence. If you are torn about a question and can't decide between two answers, you're best approach is to pick one and move on. The longer you struggle, the more confusing it will become and the more your confidence will suffer.

Jeff Says:

During the MBE I encountered a criminal law question I prepared for. It was a "defense" question based on "Mistake of Fact," and I recognized the issue immediately. The fact pattern involved a man who committed a larceny and one answer choice was that he would be innocent if his mistake was "reasonable" and the other was that the mistake was "honest." I immediately felt inclined to pick that the man would be acquitted of a larceny charge if his mistake was "honest," but something pulled me back. I knew that the test for "Mistake of Fact" depended upon

150

whether or not the crime charged was a specific or general intent crime. I knew that larceny was a specific intent crime, but I couldn't remember if that meant his mistake needed to be "reasonable" or merely "honest." I spent seven minutes on this question. It was a complete disaster. My confidence wavered; I became confused and nervous and was still nowhere closer to remembering the right answer when I finally made my choice. At the last second, I went against my instincts and selected "reasonable." I had chosen the wrong answer. With a specific intent crime, one's mistake only needs to be honest because that will negate the mens rea or specific intent required to be guilty of that crime. This is a subjective test. A mistake with a general intent crime, however, such as a battery or rape, needs to be honest and reasonable, which is an objective test. Needless to say, I never forgot the "Mistake of Fact" rule again. However, I wasted valuable time in which I could have been focusing on questions that I had a better chance of answering correctly.

The lesson here is simple – don't spend too long on a single question and don't get emotional about a particular question either. You may have spent a considerable amount of time studying the "entrapment defense," but if you are blanking out on the rule, don't waste time obsessing over it. Just move on. If you prefer, write down the question number on a piece of scratch paper and return to it later on if you have a few minutes to spare at the end of the test section.

B. AFTER A DAY

Steve says:

After taking the first day of the bar exam, I mostly remembered those questions that for the life of me had at least two correct answers. Impossible questions in areas I had taught bugged me even more. I knew that holding on to these questions was not a smart move – I was carrying the questions around long after the questions were over. I've learned to let these questions go and stay present during exams. I try to follow Yogi Berra's advice: "When you see a fork in the road, take it." (and keep looking straight ahead)

If you're taking the entire bar exam, you've most likely just finished the state part of the exam and you are probably exhausted. You have walked directly back to your hotel room and collapsed on top of your well-made bed, lying atop your comforter, staring at the hotel room ceiling. You immediately wonder what other people put down for their answers. You may feel tempted to ask your friends how they answered questions. If you engage in this risky conduct, do so only with intellectual curiosity. Don't start worrying if their answers differed from your own or they wrote something in their essay that you forgot. They may be wrong, and even if they're right, there's no way you can figure out whether you passed from memory. It's impossible.

Your best bet now is to engage in an activity for a little while that is completely non-bar related. Try not to go to sleep if you think it's going to hinder your ability to crash later on. You would be well served to get a good dinner, preferably in your room or away from other bar students. Their fear may be contagious. If the hotel has a pool or a workout room, go for it. You may want to invite a friend over for a movie. The most studying you should engage in is reviewing your multistate flash cards and anchor words. You need to refresh your multistate memory chips, so studying some of the law is probably worthwhile. Hopefully, you're tired enough to get a good night's sleep. When it's finally time and you're ready to click off the light, go ahead. Let it go.

C. AFTER THE EXAM

The Multistate exam conditions won't be any different than the state part of your exam and vice-versa, so we won't bore you by repeating the previous part. By 4:30 p.m. you likely will be finished with the MBE and thus finished with your bar exam adventure. There's only one part left and we strongly recommend it. It's time to celebrate.

If you're someone who likes company, plan to go out with classmates. Go spend some time with your friends. If you want to take it easy, there may be a better remedy that's more relaxing and low-key, like watching your favorite show on T.V.

It's important that you reward yourself whether it's the night you finish the exam or the night afterwards. This has been a considerable, taxing experience and it's good to feel a sense of closure for this chapter of your life. It will help you move forward, mentally and emotionally, so that you feel a healthy sense of completion.

One quicksand trap that many bar-takers fall into is that they begin to obsess over bar questions after the exam. This is extremely common and almost unavoidable. We don't recommend it, but since one of the authors (guess who) is guilty of this charge, we won't get down on you for it. It's not uncommon to call all your friends and ask them what they put for a particular lengthy and memorable Constitutional Law fact pattern or a strange and confusing Contracts question (even providing the number of the question). You may have even encountered a couple of questions in which you couldn't figure out exactly which subject area you were in – the new "hybrid question" fact pattern. Hopefully, you were able to figure it out by applying the framework. If you weren't, hopefully your instincts drew you to the right answer.

It's very common to sit around wondering whether or not you answered dozens of questions correctly. Although you may be able to reconstruct some of them in your head and check with your friends or professors, there are three problems you should be aware of concerning this process. One, the answers are subjective, so even if your professor thinks that one answer is correct, the bar examiners may have viewed it differently in terms of what the "best answer" was. Two, unless you remember the entire fact pattern, verbatim, there may have been a small

153

word somewhere that changed the legal outcome and thus the correct answer. Three, there are dozens of easy questions you got right, but you're not going to remember these because they weren't very distinguishable. Chances are, you're remembering the hard ones and the bizarre ones and you may find that you got some of them wrong. Don't judge your chances of passing based on these more unusual questions. There's a high probability that everyone else found those questions challenging as well (maybe even impossible). If most people got them wrong, they may award credit for multiple answers.

Our advice: Just take it easy. Take a vacation in Hawaii, or, if you really want to, now you can really go to Vegas. Now, it's okay to go there and roll the dice all you want. Whatever you do, let the bar exam go. It's time for you to enjoy your life for a while. You've survived one of the most intense studying processes in the world. You should be proud of yourself.

OK, **READY?** – It's time to move on and practice law!

XIII. <u>THE WORKBOOK CHAPTER: APPLYING YOUR KNOWLEDGE</u>

Although it's useful for us to describe in broad terms what we mean by "studying smart" and using active techniques, it's a heckuva lot more helpful to demonstrate what we're preaching to you. Students learn to worship outlines and start to believe that they are the keys to the magic kingdom of success. In reality, however, even the best outlines focus mainly on the first step of the learning process, which is content-knowledge. Outlines don't provide a path to the proper execution (meaning application or method-knowledge) of the knowledge you learn. This execution, or application, of knowledge – which is really critical reading, thinking and writing – is essential to passing the bar exam. It's like buying all of the right ingredients for a great meal but not knowing how to cook them. (Many students who go astray in their studying often don't even know they are heading in the wrong direction.) So this is the workbook chapter – we've told you what to do and now we're going to give you the opportunity to try it out.

We called this chapter a "workbook chapter" because it is primarily centered around you, the reader, actively working through problems. It's not about you being a passive observer. You are the "doer," the "decider". To check how you are doing, the answers to the problems are located in the back of the chapter.

Every course has its own issues and is organized differently. Students have greater affinity to some courses as compared to others. In a sense, it's very similar to languages – it's a lot easier to learn some languages as compared to others. For instance, Spanish probably is easier to learn than Mandarin Chinese. You might really hate a course and have a natural aversion to it, but this chapter offers some ways to unlock the

155

mysteries of courses so each one can be interesting as well as challenging.

Another reason for this workbook chapter is that to really understand the components of a course, it is not enough to just read about it. That's like taking an auto mechanic's course and watching films of auto mechanics repairing cars. Sure, that's helpful, but it won't help you become the expert – and that's the goal for the bar exam. So, this chapter is more about you taking the car apart and putting it back together to get the real feel for what the auto mechanic must do.

CONTRACTS

Contracts has a number of intricate rules. It's easy to get lost in the rules and forget about the big picture of contracts – the basic order, or steps, of solving contracts questions. That's why, when you're working in contracts, it is really, really helpful to keep the overall contracts framework in mind – make it second-nature – and then to learn the location of all the little pieces within the framework. At a minimum, it is very useful to understand the differences between the U.C.C. and the common law.

A. The Basic Protocol

Overall, contracts has a protocol that is fairly simple when compared to the multiplicity of rules and positions that are contained within the basic contracts course. The steps to a contracts question – not covering everything, such as quasi-contract, which has its own protocol – are as follows:

Overall Contracts Framework

1. Which law applies, U.C.C. or Common Law?

2. Was there a Contract?

3. Was there a Breach of Contract?

4. Are there any Defenses?

5. What remedy is appropriate?

B. Where are the Following Contracts "Pieces" <u>Located</u> in the Overall Contracts Framework?

1. Statute of Frauds

_____

[Free Advice: Don't just see Statute of Frauds issues every time you have a contracts problem. And don't just deal with it first.]

2. Conditions

_____

[Free Advice: Conditions are usually associated with a larger contracts issue. Location is very important to this issue.]

3. Unilateral vs. Bilateral

[Free Advice: Unilateral contracts do not arise without some clear indication the promise made was to be exchanged for performance.]

_____.

C. Compare

Compare U.C.C. and Common Law in Major Areas

[Free Advice: Knowing the difference between U.C.C. and CL can get you a couple of points pretty quickly, if only because the test-creators love to blend both sets of rules in the options for a single multiple choice question. Be warned - Fail to understand the distinctions at your own risk.]

Modification:

_____

_____

_____

_____

Options and the firm offer rule:

_____

_____

_____

_____

Acceptance:

_____

_____

_____

_____

Acceptance of nonconforming goods:

_____

_____

_____

_____

<u>Big Contracts question #1</u>: Does the U.C.C. or common law apply? [What matters is why this is the first question to ask and not whether a contract exists.]
When does the U.C.C. apply?

_____

_____

Too many students respond to contracts questions by first asking whether a contract existed. That's an important question to ask, but it's actually the SECOND question they should be asking. FIRST, they need to determine whether the U.C.C. or Common Law applies to the case at hand.

[Free Advice: The more problems you can do to "transfer" your knowledge from one fact variation to another, the more skilled you will be in that subject.]

<u>HYPOTHETICAL QUESTION</u> (Please write out your answer.) Jones says he will paint Smith's house on December 18th at 9 a.m. for $5,000, provided that Smith leaves the paint out in front of the house by 9 am on the 18th. Smith agrees and

they shake hands on it. Jones shows up to paint on the appointed day by 9 a.m., but there's no paint out front and he doesn't paint. Smith sues Jones for not painting. Who will win? (You can use the sample framework.) _____

Sample Contract Framework

a. Which law applies, U.C.C. or Common Law?

b. Was there a Contract?

c. Was there a Breach of Contract?

d. Are there any Defenses?

e. What Remedy is appropriate?

_____

_____

_____

_____

_____

_____

_____

_____

_____

_____

Applying Your Knowledge

_____

_____

_____

_____

_____

_____

_____

_____

_____

_____

_____

_____

_____

_____

_____

_____

_____

The Workbook Chapter

_____

_____

_____

_____

_____

_____

_____

_____

_____

_____

_____

_____

_____

_____

_____

_____

_____

_____

_____

_____

_____

_____

_____

_____

_____

_____

EVIDENCE

A. The Basic Protocol and Some Comparisons

Evidence is a course with some very big intersections that must be navigated properly. Winging it tempts a whole slew of wrong turns and lots of Las Vegas-style guessing, making Evidence one of the most difficult subjects tested on the bar exam.

The Evidence questions are usually short – but jam-packed with information. A single sentence could be packed with crucial legal information, with multiple parties and a variety of issues. A single question, for example, could start out as a Torts issue, turn into relevance and then end up as a subsequent remedial measure. The questions don't offer a lot of time for deliberation or reflection, either, which of course, exponentially increases their difficulty.

1. A Protocol (Blueprint or Roadmap) for Answering Evidence Questions on the Bar Exam

Big Question #1: To what is the evidence relevant? [There are at least three major possibilities.]

_____

_____

One Major Answer to Big Question #1: Proving Issues in the Case

      Evidence offered to prove an issue in the case covers several major topics. These areas are Relevance, Character, Opinion, Hearsay, Privilege and Writings. Understanding the differences – and being able to compare them – matter a lot in answering evidence questions on the bar exam.

    a. <u>Relevance</u>: What are some of the important relevance issues?

_____

_____

_____

_____

b. Character Evidence: What is character evidence and how does it compare to impeachment evidence? These are two important questions that the evidence guru must be able to answer.

_____

_____

_____

_____

_____

c. Opinions: Expert and lay (non-expert) - When is a witness considered an expert?

_____

_____

_____

1. If an expert witness is offered, what is the standard of reliability under the Federal Rules of Evidence?

_____

_____

_____

2. What kinds of issues are the proper subject of expert testimony?

---

3. Can expert testimony be based on inadmissible hearsay?

---

d. <u>Hearsay</u>

1. What is hearsay?

---

2. What out-of-court statements are not offered for the truth of the matter asserted?

---

3. What evidence meets all of the elements of hearsay but is not hearsay according to the Federal Rules?

_____

_____

_____

e. <u>Privilege</u>

1. What law governs federal privileges?

_____

_____

_____

2. When do state privileges apply in federal court?

_____

_____

_____

3. What are some significant federal privileges?

_____

_____

_____

f. <u>Writings</u>: While this is not often taught as a separate category in law school, writings give rise to three areas of objections – Hearsay, Authentication and the Best Evidence Rule. Understanding how these might arise is very important to the test-taker, so let's give it a shot.

1. When will a writing be hearsay?

_____

_____

_____

2. When will a writing invoke the best evidence rule?

_____

_____

_____

3. When will a writing have to be authenticated?

_____

_____

2. Illustrating Deep Understanding: Admissions

To get deep understanding of a rule, there must be mastery. This includes knowledge of the elements, brief explanations of each element, examples, exceptions (or exclusions) and, last but not least, comparisons. What follows is a brief foray into the road to understanding admissions by a party opponent.

a. A Type of "Non Hearsay"

Admissions is one of those areas where students have a vague understanding of a subject, but not a solid, precise and concise grasp. That's why the bar examiners love to test it.

Students not only have to know the location of a subject, but also some key words that allow the subject to be rapidly accessed and applied. Admissions generally are party statements that must be offered by opposing parties, across the "v." So the source of the statements and who is offering the statements matter a lot, but whether anything is actually admitted by the party is irrelevant.

b. Admissions by a party-opponent

Many students are confused by admissions and there's a good reason why. Admissions are essentially statements made by a PARTY opponent offered against the opposing party. Unlike the rest of admissible hearsay, there is no assurance of reliability in these statements. They can be backward looking, speculative and have other indicators that suggest a lack of believability. Admissions, however, are permitted for a whole different reason – if a party made the statement, let that party explain it. In other words, we're not looking at the reliability of the statement as much as we are how the statement reflects on the party who said it. Thus, the admissibility of admissions is more a matter of the judicial process than a technical assurance of the statement's worth.

Elements:

a. Statement by a party

b. Offered by the party-opponent – meaning?

_____

_____

Which rules of evidence do not apply to admissions?

_____

_____

_____

Compare to Statements Against Interest (SAI) – What are the differences?

_____

_____

_____

- SAI or Admissions do not require unavailability of the declarant?

_____

- SAI or Admissions need not be against the maker's interest?

_____

- SAI or Admissions are made by parties or their vicarious proxies?

  _____

- SAI or Admissions are not hearsay?

  _____

<u>Types of Admissions</u>: There are 5 types of admissions – two are personal and three are vicarious.

    <u>Type #1: Personal Statements</u>:
    These kinds of statements are made by?

    _____

    _____

    _____

    <u>Type #2: Adoptive Admissions</u>:
    These are not made expressly by parties. This type means?

    _____

    _____

    _____

<u>Representative (vicarious) statements</u>: These admissions are not made by the party herself, but by others. They can be offered against the party just like any statements made by the party.

1. <u>Type #3: Authorized Admissions</u>:
   This type means?

_____

_____

_____

2. <u>Type #4: Agency Admissions</u>
   This type means?

_____

_____

_____

3. How is an agency admission distinct from
   authorized admissions?

_____

_____

4. <u>Type #5: Co-conspirator admissions</u>
   This type means?

_____

_____

   a. What is a coconspirator?

_____

_____

b. What are the prerequisites for co-conspirator statements?

_____

_____

c. Is a charge of conspiracy necessary?

_____

_____

d. What type of evidence is needed?

_____

_____

e. How much evidence is required?

_____

_____

B. *Crawford v. Washington, 541 U.S. 36 (2004)* **and the Confrontation Clause: Adding Some More Depth**

In 2006, Justice Scalia and the U.S. Supreme Court shook up the analysis of the Confrontation Clause of the 6th Amendment. The Court gave it teeth, disallowing some hearsay statements offered against the accused in criminal cases. Justice Scalia said the key was whether testimonial hearsay was being offered against an accused without the opportunity for cross-examination. Prosecutors around the country cried. Evidence courses – and the bar exam – adjusted accordingly. The Confrontation Clause now had teeth.

1. Source: _____ Amendment Right to confront witnesses against D in a criminal case

2. *Old analysis*: Firmly _____ hearsay exception = presumptive reliability of statements. Admit.

3. *New analysis*: "Testimonial" hearsay assertions, no matter how firmly rooted, are admissible only if the defendant had a prior opportunity to do what?

_____

_____

4. Testimonial statements include affidavits, statements that are the product of custodial interrogation by police, depositions, courtroom testimony and "statements that were made under circumstances which would lead _____
_____ to believe that the statement would be available for use at a later trial."

CONSTITUTIONAL LAW

Constitutional law can be divided up into three main areas – Court's jurisdiction; powers of government; and rights. Obviously, you must know you weren't going to get away with something that simple, so, of course, each of these areas has sub-issues. Constitutional Law is not inscrutable if you develop a solid understanding of the frameworks and it is often the highest scored area on the bar exam. We strongly advise you to take advantage of this possibility and master it to the best of your ability.

1. **Court's Jurisdiction:** Often called justiciability. This area asks whether the court has the power to hear the case. Sub-issues include standing, political questions, mootness and ripeness.

2. **Powers of Government:** This category often takes a back seat to rights – except of course in basic constitutional law classes and on the bar exam. There are numerous powers of the legislature, (meaning Congress, state and municipal governments), Executive Branch, and _____

   _____.

3. **Rights:** The rights category limits governmental action.

   a. Which rights limit only the federal government?

   _____

   _____

   b. Which rights limit only state governments?

   _____

   _____

c. Which rights limit both federal and state governments?

_____

_____

THE 11TH AMENDMENT: A SUE-FREE ZONE FOR STATES

One area that overlaps the Court's Jurisdiction and the Powers of Government is the 11th Amendment. That Amendment prohibits a citizen of a state from sometimes suing a state (her own or another) **in federal court**. This immunity from suit is not absolute. The Eleventh Amendment does not bar suits when:

1. _____;

2. **United States is suing states**;

3. **States** _____;

4. Congress is relying on its **14th Amendment, Section 5** power

5. Suits against **municipalities, counties or cities**;

6. Suits against **state officials** for violations of _____ or other _____ where:

    a. Injunctive or declaratory relief is sought
    b. Prospective payments of state funds are sought
    c. Damages are sought against the state official personally, or

d. Only _____ are awarded (even where payable by the state).

7. Suits in State Court

a. Exception: **Sovereign Immunity Concept** (*Alden v. Maine*, 527 U.S. 706 (1999))

THE COMMERCE CLAUSE: A HUGE FEDERAL POWER (AND STILL GROWING)

Article I, Section 8, Clause 3 (known as the "Commerce Clause") grants to Congress the power to **regulate interstate commerce.**

An act of Congress attempting to regulate interstate commerce will be upheld if it can be rationally construed as a regulation of:

1. The _____ of interstate commerce;

2. The **instrumentalities** of interstate commerce;

3. Or activities that may have **substantial affects** on interstate commerce.

- Channels include the _____

_____;

- Instrumentalities include _____

_____;

- Substantial affects often has far-reaching implications. Congress may regulate activities that, in the

_____, might reasonably produce a substantial (generally economic) effect on interstate commerce.

- MNEMONIC: **ICSA** *LOPEZ*

- ICSA stands for what Congress can regulate: **I**nstrumentalities; **C**hannels; and **S**ubstantial **E**ffects on interstate commerce. Lopez is the seminal case creating the modern rules.

United States v. Lopez, 514 U.S. 549 (1995) is the reigning important Supreme Court case in the area. In *Lopez*, the Supreme Court struck down a federal criminal law that prohibited the possession of a firearm within 1,000 feet of a school.

Famous Problem: A farmer grows a small amount of wheat on 23 acres, primarily for personal use. Could Congress regulate this farmer's wheat under the Commerce Clause? Why?

■■

While it is not often looked on as a power, the judiciary's power to hear cases and controversies, alternatively called jurisdiction, is an important power.

a. **Federal Court Jurisdiction**

    1. What is the jurisdiction of the federal courts?

    _____

    _____

    _____

2. What limits can Congress make over that jurisdiction?

_____

_____

_____

3. When does Congress go too far?

_____

_____

_____

Rights (and limits)

DORMANT COMMERCE CLAUSE

The so-called "dormant" commerce clause functions as a limit on state powers over commerce. Distinction: How is the Dormant Commerce Clause (also known as the negative implications of the Commerce Clause) different from the Commerce Clause?

_____

_____

_____

Conflict

Because Congress has the lawful power to regulate interstate commerce, any state regulations that conflict with valid Congressional acts will be unconstitutional. Why?

_____

_____

_____

Preemption

Because the Commerce Clause gives Congress _____ to regulate interstate commerce, Congress may elect to _____ the ability of the states to regulate interstate commerce. Congress may enact regulations that _____ preempt all state regulations **relating to** the same subject matter.

State Regulations Discriminating Against Interstate Commerce

Even if there is no conflict or preemption, generally states may not **discriminate** against interstate commerce. What do we mean when we say 'discriminate' against interstate commerce? We're talking about 'protectionist' laws that promote the State's economy over the economic interests of other states. For example, if California taxed all oranges imported into the State but not oranges grown in-state, that could be a discriminatory regulation. When a state statute discriminates against interstate commerce, either **on its face** or in _____, the burden falls upon the state to show a legitimate purpose being served and the unavailability of nondiscriminatory alternatives sufficient to protect the local interest.

- Discrimination defined: the state regulation treats interstate commerce more adversely than local, in-state commerce.
- The exception: _____.

Market Participant Exception

The Supreme Court has upheld discriminatory state regulations when the state acts as a _____.

Famous Problem (Supreme Court Case): A South Dakota law requiring all cement produced by a state-owned cement plant to be sold locally. Is this constitutional under a Commerce Clause challenge? Yes, because South Dakota was acting as a seller in the marketplace and could favor in-state business.

Burden Analysis

Even if state laws do not discriminate against interstate commerce, states also cannot impose an _____ on interstate commerce. This means that if a state regulation is not preempted by federal law and does not discriminate against interstate commerce, the regulation will be held invalid if it imposes an _____ on interstate commerce.

Courts will balance the burden imposed on interstate commerce against the local interest advanced by the state law.

Famous Problem: Can a state limit all trucks' mud flaps to a special contour design?

EQUAL PROTECTION

Quick Tips About Equal Protection (and government classification)

- Expressly found in 14th Amendment (limiting States); implied in _____ Amendment Due Process (limiting the Federal government)

- Guarantees equal treatment, not equal rights

- It has to be the **government or one of its agents acting** to trigger equal protection, not private persons or entities (*i.e.,* look for "state action")

- Two broad areas in which equal protection applies:
  o **(1) Government classifications** and **(2) fundamental rights**
  o Basic mantra for what equal protection means when the government classifies: "Similarly situated people must be treated similarly."

Classification in the "**Pyramid Protection Plan**" determines the level of scrutiny a law must survive to be held constitutional.

- Top of the Pyramid(three really suspect classifications) <u>RAN</u>:
  _____ – Strict Scrutiny

- Middle of the Pyramid(two somewhat suspect classifications): <u>GNMC</u>:
  _____ Scrutiny

- Top of the Bottom of the Pyramid: <u>RBWB (Rational Basis with a Bite)</u>: **Mental Disability or Sexual Orientation – Strong Rational Basic Scrutiny**

- <u>All Other Classifications</u>: Rational Basis Scrutiny

Standards of Review

The court employs _____ **primary standards** of review to determine whether the government action impermissibly discriminates:

1. **<u>Strict Scrutiny</u>**: Government action which intentionally discriminates against a _____ or violates a **"fundamental right"** will be subject to strict scrutiny.

   Unless the government can demonstrate that its actions are _____ to achieve a _____ government interest, the action will be unconstitutional.

2. **<u>Intermediate Scrutiny</u>:** Certain types of discrimination are examined under an **intermediate** level of scrutiny – less than "strict scrutiny" but greater than "rational basis" scrutiny The test is: the government must demonstrate its actions are _____ to achieve a _____ government interest.

3. **<u>Rational Basis Test</u>:** The vast majority of state and federal laws creating classifications are tested under "rational basis" scrutiny. Here, social and economic legislation is _____ and will be upheld by the Court unless the challenger can meet its burden of showing the law or government action is not _____ related to a _____ government interest.

To Satisfy –

Strict Scrutiny: The law must be _____ related to a _____ governmental interest.

Intermediate Scrutiny: The law must be _____ related to an _____ governmental interest.

Rational Basic Scrutiny: The law must be **rationally** related to a **legitimate** governmental interest.

CRITICAL WRITING:
WHAT TO DO AND WHAT NOT TO DO

PROPERTY ESSAY (50 Minutes)

Oliver Owney owned an estate of approximately 350 acres outside of Greensboro. The tract was located in a hilly and picturesque area and was surrounded by trees, with the exception of the east side, which fronted a spring-fed lake. The north 5 acres had a large house on it, a guest quarters, and a stream running through it. The border on the west side of the property fronted a narrow, 50-yard forest, which divided the property from a housing development of big 5 and 6 bedroom homes, each on an acre of land. Alice Patterson lived in the neighborhood that abutted Owney's land on the west side.

In 1997, Alice began training for the New York Marathon. Because running on streets bothered her knees, Alice would jog on the outside 10 yards of the forest on Owney's property, through the trees. She sometimes cleared the trees on her jogging path and made the ground suitable for running. The views were spectacular, so in a place that was not easily seen from Owney's house or any nearby road, Alice installed a hammock between two trees for napping and just looking at the sky. She took naps infrequently. The hammock was a piece of canvas strung between two trees, with a mat underneath, an all-weather pillow, a wooden step, wooden guardrails and branches partially covering the hammock, giving it an enclosed feeling. Once or twice a year, Alice even slept in the hammock overnight, just to see the beautiful night sky.

Oliver was strongly allergic to poison ivy, which grew in abundance in the forest. While he vaguely observed what Alice was doing during one of his daily walks, he shunned the forested areas of his property because of his allergy.

One day in 1999, Oliver's dog escaped from the house and headed to the back of the property where Alice's hammock was located. Oliver caught the dog right on the perimeter of his property. Alice was heading toward the area at that exact moment, ready to take a jog. Oliver started talking with Alice, in full view of the hammock. He found out she was training for the marathon, smiled, and said, "Good luck." Oliver added, "Nice hammock; you just need a better roof," and turned to leave. As he was leaving, he yelled, "Just don't jog on my property; there's a lot of poison ivy on it." Alice ignored the warning and kept on jogging on Oliver's property. In 1999, Oliver began walking as exercise and would use Alice's jogging path, but they didn't run into each other.

Alice exercised weekly through November 2005. At that time, Alice hurt her leg and stopped using "the track," as she called Owney's land. After her leg healed three months later, she started up again, even taking naps in the hammock. Soon after, Owney decided to sell his property and move to Florida. Owney realized he would have to do something about Alice first, so he filed an ejectment action in early 2006.

A) *What is the best argument Alice can advance in the lawsuit to permit her to continue using Owney's land?*

[Don't panic – try to briefly explain. We'll go over a good sample answer later on.] (30 minutes)

B) Will Alice likely Prevail? Why? (20 minutes)

<u>Note</u>: Assume the statute of limitations for adverse possession, prescriptive easements and other prescriptive claims in the jurisdiction is 8 years by claim of right and 6 years by color of title.

_____

_____

_____

_____

_____

_____

_____

_____

_____

_____

_____

_____

Applying Your Knowledge

_____

_____

_____

_____

_____

_____

_____

_____

_____

_____

_____

_____

_____

_____

_____

_____

_____

_____

_____

_____

_____

_____

_____

_____

_____

_____

_____

_____

_____

_____

_____

_____

Applying Your Knowledge

_____

_____

_____

_____

_____

_____

_____

_____

_____

_____

_____

_____

_____

_____

_____

_____

_____

_____

_____

_____

_____

_____

_____

_____

_____

_____

_____

_____

_____

WORKBOOK CHAPTER - ANSWERS AND EXPLANATIONS

CONTRACTS

B. Where are the following contracts "pieces" located in the overall framework?

1. **Statute of Frauds:** It goes in the defenses section, unless a contract is defined as offer, acceptance, consideration and no valid defenses. Without the requisite writing required by the statute, the agreement is voidable, not void.

2. **Conditions:** These are located in the category of "Breach of Contract." Conditions trigger performance. This means generally that if a condition is not met, performance is not required.

3. **Unilateral vs. bilateral:** This dichotomy is located in the contracts formation section of the framework. This distinction describes the difference between a promise for action (unilateral) and a promise for a promise. Too many students construe ambiguous offers as offers for action, not as a promise in return for a promise. There should be a clear indication that the agreement is a promise for performance and not a promise in return of a promise.

C. Compare

Compare U.C.C. and Common Law in Major Areas

Modification:

CL: A modification of a contract generally required consideration, especially to avoid the preexisting duty rule.

UCC: Under 2-209, good faith modifications generally do not require consideration. However, the Statute of Frauds applies.

Options and the Firm Offer Rule:

CL: Under the CL, a mere promise to keep an offer open is revocable. If the offer includes consideration, however, it may be binding. Note that under a unilateral contract, an option is created by an offeree who commences performance.

UCC: (UCC 2-205) Under the UCC, an offer can be held firm – without consideration – for a reasonable period up to three months. That does not mean an offer cannot be held open longer than three months, just that three months is the maximum time it must be maintained without being subject to revocation.

Acceptance:

CL: Assent must occur for each and every term of the offer. Any modification, such as additional or different terms, creates a rejection of the offer, and is instead replaced by a counteroffer.

UCC: Under 2-606, acceptance occurs when the buyer indicates as such or simply does not reject the goods after a reasonable time period. The buyer must first have a reasonable opportunity to inspect the goods. If additional terms are included by the offeree, those are considered mere proposals.

Acceptance of Nonconforming Goods:
Under the U.C.C., acceptance of nonconforming goods is treated as an acceptance and a breach of the offeror's promise. It promotes continuity in the marketplace, while protecting the accepting party's rights. A buyer may reject all non-conforming goods, accept all or accept any commercial unit of goods.

Big question #1: Does the U.C.C. or common law apply? The answer, of course, is the U.C.C. applies to the sale of goods. In contracts questions, it is first important to determine what the applicable law is – because the legal rule determines the answer. In multiple choice questions, in particular, it is very easy for the examiners to pack the responses with both common law and U.C.C. answers.

Why is this big question #1? This question comes first because it fixes the applicable law. The U.C.C. and the common law overlap, but are certainly not identical. Applying the correct law is step #1.

[Too many students start off contracts asking whether a contract existed in the first place. As we said before, that's the second question. It is first important to determine whether the U.C.C. or CL applies to the case at hand. This will help you avoid a lot of confusing problems later on that cause people to choose the wrong answer choice.]

HYPOTHETICAL QUESTION (Please write out your answer). Jones says he will paint Smith's house on December 18th for $5,000 provided that Smith leaves the paint out in front of the house by 9 am on the 18th. Smith said yes. Jones shows up to paint on the appointed day, but there's no paint out front and he doesn't paint. Smith sues Jones.

Who will win? The scaffolding you should generally use for a contracts question follows:

a. <u>Which law applies, U.C.C. or CL?</u>
[The focus here should be on whether the relationship between the parties involves a sale of goods – not simply whether there were merchants involved.] Since the contract was for a service, painting a house, and not a sale of goods, the common law applies.

b. <u>Was there a Contract?</u>
A contract requires an offer, acceptance and consideration.

1. Here, there was an offer because Jones offered to paint Smith's house for $5,000.

2. Here, there was an acceptance because Smith said yes to Jones' inquiry.

3. Here, consideration was also present because each party was to receive something of value, Smith a house with a fresh coat of paint and Jones money.

c. <u>Was there a Breach of Contract?</u>
A breach of contract involves some form of nonperformance of obligations under a contract by a party. Conditions generally trigger performance.

Here, there was a condition precedent of placing the paint outside the front of the house. Before Jones painted, Smith was required to meet this condition. Because Smith did not place the paint at the front of the house on the day in question, Jones' obligation to paint was not triggered and Jones did not breach his contractual obligation.

d. Are there any Defenses?
The Statute of Frauds is a defense to contractual obligations. It applies to the sale of goods and the U.C.C., but not service contracts. Here, the Statute of Frauds does not apply because the contract is a service contract to paint a house, not a sale of goods. There appears to be no other defense that can be reasonably asserted.

e. What remedy is appropriate?
There are various remedies for breach of contract when a party fails to fulfill its obligations. These measures include restitution, expectation damages, rescission and specific performance. Here, there was no breach of contract by Jones the painter and thus no remedies are appropriate.

Wrong turn: **Unilateral Contract** - This doctrinal area may be tempting, but don't go there unless there is evidence that the parties intended an agreement that exchanged a promise for performance.

Wrong turn: **Statute of Frauds** - the Statute of Frauds is not relevant here because the contract involves a service - painting - and not the sale of goods.

EVIDENCE

A. The Basic Protocol and Some Comparisons

1. A Protocol (Blueprint or Roadmap) for Answering Evidence Questions on the Bar Exam

Big Question #1: **To what is the evidence relevant?**
[There are at least three major possibilities – proving an
issue in the case, impeaching a witness or both.]

In short, the "relevant to what" question is
asking whether the evidence is relevant to proving an
issue in the case, impeaching a witness or both. This
question has to be asked over and over again until it is
second nature.

Proving issues in the case can mean a question is
directed at providing evidence of an element of the cause
of action, claim or defense. There are several categories
that such evidence falls within. These include relevance,
character, opinion, hearsay, privilege, witnesses and
writings.

Proving Issues In the Case

a. Relevance: What are some of the important
    relevance issues?

    Relevance really means, in its basic form,
    helpfulness to the jury. When is relevant evidence
    excluded? When it is unfairly prejudicial and for
    other policy reasons, such as when the evidence is a
    subsequent remedial measure or an offer to
    compromise or plead guilty or the like as well.

b. Character Evidence: What is character evidence and
    how it compares to impeachment evidence are two
    important questions that the evidence guru must be
    able to answer.

    Character and Impeachment both involve trait or
    disposition evidence (*e.g.,* once a thief, always a
    thief....). Impeachment, however, is generally only

196

about a single trait – the witness' credibility, also called the witness' character for truthfulness.

Character is about the trait relevant to issues in the case, namely, what the elements of the case require. Another important distinction is that impeachment is only about witnesses. It is not proper unless and until someone takes the witness stand (or does the functional equivalent, as with hearsay declarants). Character evidence, on the other hand, is about the parties or victims (not witnesses!). Look for direct use to prove character of a party or other person when it is an element in a case (such as defamation cases) or indirect use to help prove issues in case.

QUICK DISTINCTION SUMMARY:

Character is generally for parties (and victims) – concerns a trait or disposition relevant to the case. Impeachment is for witnesses – generally referring to truthfulness (and accuracy), another way of saying a witness's character for truthfulness.

c.   Opinions – Expert and lay (non-expert) –

When is a witness considered an expert?

Qualifying the witness as an expert in a particular field is only one of the prerequisites to testifying as an expert. The theory underlying the science or basis of the testimony must be reliable, as must the applications of that science or field of study.

1. What is the standard for reliability of the scientific, technical or experiential basis of the expert testimony?

All experts must be screened by judges to ensure a reliable theory and reliable application. If an expert witness is offered, does the testimony satisfy the Rule 702 reliable science standard? Rule 702 adopted the multiple factor test advanced in *Daubert v. Merrill Dow Pharmaceuticals*, 509 U.S. 579 (1993). The approach was expanded to rest on a variety of factors. The judge uses these factors to determine if the science or field is sufficiently reliable to permit the testimony.

2. What kinds of issues are the proper subject of expert testimony?

Students too often confuse qualification of experts and other expert testimony issues. The kinds of issues that an expert may testify about can be defined within the context of relevance – any relevant issue, even the ultimate issue, can be the subject of expert testimony.

Of course, there are some limitations.

The expert's testimony must be helpful and cannot, in a criminal case at least, opine whether the accused had the mental state necessary to commit the crime. (This is the so-called Hinckley Rule of the Federal Rules of Evidence, 704(b), to prevent dueling psychotherapists directly wrestling with the issue of mental state.)

REMEMBER: AN EXPERT CAN NOT GIVE HER DIRECT OPINION ON A CRIMINAL DEFENDANT'S MENTAL STATE.

3. Can expert testimony be based on inadmissible hearsay?

The answer here is yes, so long as the testimony is **reasonably relied on** in the particular scientific field. For example, in the medical field, health care professionals regularly rely on the entries by other health care professionals (*e.g.*, doctors and nurses) in the charts.

d. Hearsay

1. What is hearsay?

There are four elements in hearsay –
(1) Out-of-court
(2) Statement
(3) By a declarant
(4) Offered for the truth of the matter asserted.

The bar examiners love testing these elements because students often do not linger over them, trying to determine what they mean. The most difficult are statements, which mean assertions of fact, and offering the statements for the truth of the matter asserted.

Everyone loves jumping right into the hearsay exceptions. There's a lot of ground to cover in the hearsay category prior to consideration of whether the evidence is reliable hearsay and thus admitted as an exception. Evidence may not be considered hearsay because it is not offered for truth.

2. <u>What statements are not offered for the</u>
<u> truth of the matter asserted</u>?

<u>This is a very difficult question because there is</u>
<u>no pat answer. The thing to keep in mind,</u>
<u>though, is that these statements are generally</u>
<u>offered for other purposes. So how they are</u>
<u>offered is critical</u>.

<u>Recurring areas of statements not offered for the</u>
<u>truth can be organized around the acronym: NO</u>
<u>PRIV, which means</u>:

1. statements offered to show **N**otice (or warning
the listener)
2. as an **O**perative fact (statement has
independent legal significance, like a contract or
will)
3. as a **P**rior inconsistent statement (offered to
impeach a witness)
4. as **R**es Gestae (completing the story)
5. to show the **I**nsanity of the declarant (and not
the truth of the outlandish statement)
and finally, a cousin to operative facts,
6. Verbal **A**cts (which help explain the legal
significance of a transfer of property, generally
as either a gift or a loan.)

DON'T FORGET: IT'S ONLY HEARSAY IF
A STATEMENT IS OFFERED FOR THE
TRUTH OF THE MATTER ASSERTED.

<u>Know that the truth of the matter asserted is not</u>
<u>the same thing as an issue in the case. Instead,</u>
<u>whether a statement is being offered for its truth</u>

depends on how it connects, how it relates, to the issues in the case.

Example

In a murder trial, the fact that a declarant arbitrarily said the accused preferred chocolate ice cream to vanilla in an out-of-court statement would probably not be considered hearsay – it had no real connection to the subject matter of the case. However, a statement by a declarant indicating where the defendant was at a particular time the killing took place would most likely qualify as hearsay because such a statement could be connected to the case – whether or not the accused is guilty or innocent of the crime for which he has been charged and thus would be offered for its truth.

Next Big Question:

3. What Statements Meet the Hearsay Definition But Still are Not Considered Hearsay By the Federal Rules of Evidence?

This question refers to special prior statements of witnesses and admissions by party opponents.

> *Location, Location, Location – in real estate and the bar exam – are keys to success.*

e. **Privileges**: This category can befuddle even the best test-takers because it is governed by Federal common law, as directed by the Federal Rules of

Evidence. In addition, the area contains hidden remnants of Civil Procedure – an Erie analysis dictates that state law rules may apply in federal court if in a diversity action the rules are considered "substantive" not "procedural."

1. What law governs federal privileges?

While the Federal Rules of Evidence are controlling, the applicable Rule 501 directs one to the federal common law. Apparently, the area was controversial enough to be left alone by the group creating the Federal Rules.

2. When do state privileges apply in federal court?

This question actually raises a civil procedure issue because when the Erie doctrine governs and state law supplies the rule of decision in federal court, substantive questions are decided by the pertinent state law. When it comes to evidence, privileges are considered substantive and state law controls. Look for diversity jurisdiction as one clue.

3. What are some significant federal privileges?

Some of the more significant federal privileges include the attorney-client privilege, the clergy-penitent privilege, the husband-wife privileges (both confidential communications and spousal immunity), and the psychotherapist-patient privilege.

f. Writings – While this is not often taught as a separate category in law school, writings give rise to three areas of objections – Hearsay, Authentication (relevancy) and the Best Evidence Rule (also called the original writings rule). Understanding how these might arise is very important to the test-taker.

1. When Will a Writing Be Hearsay?
When it meets all of the four hearsay elements (and is not a special prior statement of a witness or an admission).

2. When Will a Writing Involve the Best Evidence Rule?

Seldom. But writings that are important to a case whose contents are at issue will be subject to the rule. Think of contract, will and trust actions, where the central issue is what is in those writings.

3. When Will a Writing Have to Be Authenticated?

Everything used in court must be authenticated or "shown that it is what it purports to be" to some extent. A writing offered in evidence can be authenticated by a witness or sometimes self-authenticated.

2. Admissions – Adding Some Depth

Many students have a vague idea of what admissions are all about, but do not understand their intricacies – particularly their location in the hearsay universe. If this workbook chapter shows anything, it should be the importance of location.

a. Admissions by a party-opponent

Many students are confused by admissions. Admissions are essentially party statements offered against the opposing party. Unlike the rest of admissible hearsay, there is no assurance of reliability in these statements. They can be backward looking, speculative and have other indicators that suggest a lack of believability. Admissions, however, are permitted for a whole different reason – if a party made the statement, let that party explain it. Thus, the reliability of these statements is more a matter of the judicial process than a technical assurance of the statement's worth.

Elements: a. Statement by a party
b. Offered by the party-opponent – meaning the party across the "v" of the case. (*e.g.,* A v. B)

Which rules of evidence do not apply to admissions? The opinion rule and personal knowledge rule do not apply to admissions. The theory behind admissibility is, "You made the statement, party, now explain it." Thus the admissibility is as much about the adversary process as it is the reliability of the evidence.

Compare to Statements Against Interest (SAI) – What are the differences?

* Admissions do not require unavailability of the declarant (it is required for SAI)

* Admissions need not be against the maker's interest (it must be for SAI)

- <u>Admissions are made by parties or their vicarious proxies</u> (SAI <u>generally</u> are not)

- <u>Admissions are not hearsay</u> (SAI are hearsay exceptions)

(All four choices are admissions, not SAI)

<u>Types of Admissions</u>: There are <u>5 types</u> of admissions – two are personal and three are vicarious.

<u>Type #1: Personal Statements: Made by Whom? These kinds of statements are made by the party themselves. It could be a statement under oath or an offhand remark to a friend. The category of admissions does not differentiate between the degrees of earnestness with which the statement is made.</u>

<u>Type #2: Adoptive Admissions: Meaning? These are considered made by parties, but are initially made by another person and adopted by the party. Thus, this category includes affirmations by a party of another's assertions or even the adoption by silence. This occurs when a party does not deny an accusation that a reasonable person would deny. An example is an accusation in public that the party is having an affair. One would expect a person to deny that contention if it were not true.</u>

<u>Representative (vicarious) statements</u>: Meaning? These admissions are not made by the party themselves, but by others. They can be offered against the party just like any statements made by the party.

1. <u>Type #3</u>: <u>Authorized</u>: Meaning? <u>These statements generally emanate from a spokesperson or representative</u>

of a person or company. Celebrities have "spokespersons" – generally their publicists – and companies have similar spokespeople.

2. Type #4: Agency: Meaning? An agency admission is distinct from authorized admissions in that they are not specifically authorized by the party. Instead, these statements are made by agents of the party. Agents usually mean employees – making the party the employer – and deal with statements under special circumstances. The circumstances include statements made during the course of employment and relevant to the employment. Some independent evidence is required to show the existence of the agency relationship.

3. Type #5: Coconspirator: Meaning? The coconspirator admission category is one of the most important and least understood. It includes statements by coconspirators during and in furtherance of the conspiracy.

    a. What is a co-conspirator?

A co-conspirator is a co-felon or "partner in crime." One partner's statements may be used against the other partners by the prosecutor under certain circumstances.

A partner does not have to be present and may not know at all what his partners in crime said. That doesn't matter because the "partners" rationale governs – the party is responsible for what the partners say – and do. Charges in the case can depend on what all of the conspirators actually do.

b. What are the prerequisites of co-conspirator statements?

The "during and in furtherance" language provide two important prerequisites. Thus, statements of confession by a coconspirator are usually considered "after the fact" – after the conspiracy has ended.

c. Is a charge of conspiracy necessary?

No. It is sufficient if there is enough evidence of a conspiracy; no formal charge of conspiracy is required.

d. What type of evidence is needed?

There are quantum of proof requirements as well. The prosecutors cannot simply offer the statements of the conspiracy as proof that a conspiracy existed – a process called "bootstrapping" – but need some independent evidence as well.

e. How Much Evidence Is Required?

To prove that a conspiracy existed and that the statements were made during and in furtherance of a conspiracy, the rules dictate that a certain amount and type of evidence is required. Based on a PREPONDERANCE of the evidence pursuant to Federal Rule of Evidence 104(a), the judge will admit the evidence if there is at least some independent evidence, along with the statements offered, of those evidentiary foundations. That means a party has to offer other evidence of the conspiracy in addition to the alleged conspiratorial statements themselves.

B. *Crawford v. Washington*, **541 U.S. 36 (2004) and the Confrontation Clause – Adding Some More Depth**

1.   Source: the 6th Amendment Right to confront witnesses against D in a criminal case

2.   Old analysis: Firmly <u>rooted</u> hearsay exception = presumptive reliability

3. New analysis: "testimonial" hearsay assertions, no matter how firmly rooted, are admissible only if the defendant had a prior opportunity to cross-examine the declarant.

4. Testimonial statements include affidavits, statements that are the product of custodial interrogation by police, depositions, courtroom testimony and "statements that were made under circumstances which would lead <u>an objective witness</u> reasonably to believe that the statement would be available for use at a later trial." (*Crawford v. Washington*)

CONSTITUTIONAL LAW ISSUES: A FRAMEWORK

The basic framework of the course: *Court's Jurisdiction; Powers of Government*; **then** *Rights* **(or more expansively, Limits)**

   1. <u>Court's Jurisdiction</u>

   2. <u>Powers of Government</u> – The powers of government break down into two major divisions. Powers can be parsed vertically between Federal and State governments, the two sovereigns, called federalism.   A second way to parse the powers, horizontally, separates powers into the legislative, executive and judicial branches. These branches, particularly in the federal government, have distinct powers as defined in the Constitution.

3. Rights – The rights category limit the powers of the federal and state governments.

a. Some limit rights only limit the federal government (*e.g.*, the 10th Amendment)

b. Some only the states (e.g., the dormant commerce clause; Article IV's Privileges and Immunities Clause).

c. Some rights limit both governments, such as due process, equal protection and takings clauses.

SCOPE OF THE 11TH AMENDMENT: A SUE-FREE ZONE

A significant power for the States is the immunity from lawsuit. Part of this immunity derives from the 11th Amendment to the Constitution and part from the concept of sovereign immunity.

A citizen of one state may not sue another state, nor may a citizen sue his own state **in federal court**. The Eleventh Amendment does not bar suits when:

1. **States v. States**;
2. **United States v. States**;
3. **States consent**;
4. Congress is relying on its **14th Amendment, Section 5** power;
5. Suits against **municipalities, counties or cities**;

6. Suits against **state officials** for violations of **constitutional** or other **federal law** where:

    a. Injunctive or declaratory relief is sought

    b. Prospective payments of state funds are sought

    c. Damages are sought against the state official personally, or

    d. Only **attorney's fees** are awarded (even where payable by the state).

7. Suits in State Court

    a. Exception: **Sovereign Immunity Concept** (*Alden v. Maine,* 527 U.S. 706 (1999))

COMMERCE CLAUSE

Article I, Section 8, Clause 3 (known as the "Commerce Clause") grants to Congress the **power** to **regulate interstate commerce**. Just like Congress had the power over the jurisdiction of the inferior courts, this clause provides it with another distinct source of power – to regulate commerce between the states. The Supreme Court has offered many interpretations of what this clause means.

An act of Congress attempting to regulate interstate commerce will be upheld if it can **rationally** be construed as a regulation of:

1. The **channels** of interstate commerce,
2. The **instrumentalities** of interstate commerce,
3. Or activities that have a **substantial affect** on interstate commerce. (This last category is the most far-reaching and generally the subject of the most lawsuits.)

- Channels mean the **highways, shipping lanes, airways, etc.**

- Instrumentalities mean **planes, trains and automobiles, etc. – the things that go on or in the channels.**
- Substantial affects give Congress the greatest source of powers under this provision. Congress may regulate activities that, in the **aggregate**, might reasonably produce a substantial affect on interstate commerce, (usually an economic effect).
- MNEMONIC: **ICSE** *LOPEZ*
(ICSE = Instrumentalities, Channels and Substantial Affect; LOPEZ = the name of the major case in the area, United States v. Lopez)

In *United States v. Lopez*, 514 U.S. 549 (1995), the Supreme Court invalidated a federal criminal law that prohibited the possession of a firearm within 1,000 feet of a school. The Court reasoned that gun possession in a school zone, even when considered along with similar activity nationwide, does not have a substantial impact on interstate commerce. In the case, Justice Rehnquist set forth the modern approach, which is to assess whether the Congressional power falls within one of the three branches of the Commerce Clause – instrumentalities, channels and substantial effects – and to determine whether within substantial effects the activity is economic or substantially affects interstate commerce without heaping "inference upon inference."

Note: Even if the activity to be regulated produces only a **minor direct impact** on interstate commerce, Congress can still regulate that specific activity if **in the aggregate** with other similar activities around the nation it has a substantial impact on interstate commerce.

Famous Problem: A farmer growing 23 acres of wheat, primarily for personal use, could be regulated in his consumption by federal law. Rationale: If every small farmer was allowed to grow an unrestricted amount of wheat, even for personal consumption, the combined effect might substantially affect the national demand for, and price of, wheat. Therefore, Congress could regulate such a small amount of wheat production for personal consumption. *Wichard v. Fillburn*, 317 U.S. 111 (1942).

Federal Court Jurisdiction –

1. What is the jurisdiction of the federal courts?

The federal courts have jurisdiction over cases and controversies and are limited by the Constitution about the sources of law that supply their decision. It is mostly federal law that federal courts apply. (But see *Erie* and diversity cases, where sometimes the state law supplies the rule of decision.)

2. What limits can Congress make over that jurisdiction?

The Constitution gives the Congress power to "establish" the inferior courts - the district and appellate circuit courts - and this includes placing limits on these courts' jurisdiction.

3. When does Congress go too far?

Congress goes too far when it does not just limit court jurisdiction, but interferes in the substantive decision-making of the court. That is, rules by Congress cannot relate to fact-finding or how the courts apply the law to the facts.

DORMANT COMMERCE CLAUSE

How is the Dormant commerce Clause different than the Commerce Clause?

The Dormant Commerce Clause requires a separate analysis from Congress' Commerce Clause Powers, which often lends to student confusion. Don't let the common name, "Commerce Clause," fool you. The Dormant Commerce Clause is an implied limit on the states' power to regulate commerce. The Commerce Clause is the express power given to Congress to regulate interstate commerce in Article I, Section 8.

Conflict The Constitution and law made in pursuant thereof, especially federal laws, are the Supreme laws of the land. See Article IV, Section 2. Thus, in conflicts between valid federal and state laws, federal laws win.

Preemption

Because the federal government has **plenary power** to regulate interstate commerce, Congress may elect to **delegate, share or prohibit** the ability of the states to regulate interstate commerce. Congress may enact regulations that **expressly or impliedly** preempt all state regulations **touching upon** the same subject matter.

Tip for approaching a state regulation affecting interstate commerce: Follow this four-step analysis – 1) Is there a conflict between federal and state law? (If yes, state law loses) 2) Is the state regulation preempted by existing federal legislation on the same subject? If there is any expressed intent in the federal law or any indication, such as the pervasiveness of federal law, that Congress intended to occupy the field, then preemption occurs. 3) Does the state regulation discriminate against interstate

---

213

commerce? (Look for unequal treatment, either express or implied) 4) Does the state regulation impose an undue burden on interstate commerce? (How hurtful is it to commerce as compared to beneficial to the state?) If any of the four questions are answered in the affirmative, the state regulation is invalid.

State Regulations Discriminating Against Interstate Commerce

Absent congressional authorization, states may not **discriminate** against interstate commerce. When a state statute discriminates against interstate commerce, either **on its face** or in **practical effect**, the burden falls upon the state to essentially meet strict scrutiny and show the unavailability of nondiscriminatory alternatives sufficient to protect the local interest.

- Discrimination defined: the state regulation treats interstate commerce adversely, when compared to the treatment of local commerce.
- Important exception: **Market Participant**

Market Participant Exception

The Supreme Court has upheld discriminatory regulations enacted by states when the state acts as a **seller** or **buyer** in the marketplace.

Example: If a state law requires all cement produced by a state-owned cement plant to be sold locally, that would be permitted because the state was acting as a seller (a participant) in the marketplace, not as a regulator or "referee".

Burden Analysis

States also are restricted from imposing an **undue burden** on interstate commerce. Even if a state regulation is not preempted by federal law and does not unduly discriminate against interstate commerce, it still violates the negative implications of the commerce clause (i.e., the dormant commerce clause) if it imposes an **undue burden** on interstate commerce.

Courts will use a balancing test - balancing the burden imposed on interstate commerce against the local interest advanced by the state law.

Famous Problem:

While the state law applied to all trucks within the state, regardless of residency, the contour design for mud flaps required by the law did not provide sufficiently high benefits to justify the significant burdens in terms of extra cost and time to outfit the rigs with the new flaps.

MNEMONIC: **DIMEBA**

Mnemonic devices are very helpful to remember complicated or multi-part rules. The dormant commerce clause contains components that can be easily forgotten. Therefore, a mnemonic device is helpful: DIMEBA – (No) Discrimination in Means or Ends; even if no Burden Analysis. This mnemonic includes both parts of the doctrine – discrimination and undue burden. It also reflects that discrimination could occur through express means or implied objectives.

EQUAL PROTECTION

Quick Tips About Equal Protection

A key to understanding equal protection analysis is that it has a fork in the road – it protects against government discrimination against groups and it protects against government deprivation of several implied fundamental rights. The Equal Protection Clause's prohibition against discrimination is similar to the Dormant Commerce Clause and Privileges and Immunities Clause in that all three protect against government discrimination. Of course, the differences begin there – the dormant commerce clause and privileges and immunities clauses only protect against state discrimination, not federal government discrimination, and the types of protected discrimination are different. Equal protection protects individuals against government discrimination against groups, the privileges and immunities clause protects against discrimination against out-of-state citizens and the dormant commerce clause protects against interstate commerce discrimination. Comparisons are very useful to promote effective studying.

Quick Tips About Equal Protection (Classification)
- There's only one express clause – the 14th Amendment - expressly stated in the Constitution. The 5th Amendment Due Process Clause is considered to have an Equal Protection component.
- EP guarantees equal treatment, not equal rights
- EP applies only to **government actions, not private conduct**
- There are two broad areas where Equal Protection applies:
  Government classifications and fundamental rights
- The basic mantra for equal protection of groups is: "Similarly situated people must be treated similarly."

Classification in the **"Pyramid Protection Plan"** determines the level of scrutiny a law must survive to be held constitutional.
- RAN: **Race, Alienage and National Origin** – Strict Scrutiny – top category

- GNMC: **Gender, Non-Marital Children** – Intermediate Scrutiny – middle category
- RBWB (Rational Basis with a Bite): **Mental Disability or Sexual Orientation** – bottom category
- All Other Classes: Rational Basis – bottom category

The Equal Protection Clause of the **Fourteenth Amendment** provides that no state shall "deny to any person in its jurisdiction the equal protection of the laws."

Standards of Review

The court employs **three primary standards** of review to determine whether the government action impermissibly discriminates:

1. Strict Scrutiny – Government action, which purposely discriminates against a "**suspect class**" (or impinges upon a "**fundamental right**"), will be subject to strict scrutiny.

Unless the government can demonstrate that its actions are **necessary** to achieve a **compelling government** state interest, (i.e. the means chosen to effectuate that interest are the least restrictive action), the actions will be unconstitutional. This is the hardest test for the government to pass. If the Court applies Strict Scrutiny, there's a very high likelihood that the government will lose and that the law will be struck down or overturned.

2. Intermediate Scrutiny – Certain types of discrimination are examined under an **intermediate** level of scrutiny – less than "strict scrutiny" but greater than "rational basis." Most of the time, laws reviewed under Intermediate Scrutiny will be struck down, but it's not a guarantee. The Court demands that the law be substantially related to an important government interest.

3. Rational Basis Test – The vast majority of state and federal laws creating classifications are tested under the "rational basis" test. Here, social and economic legislation is **presumed to be constitutional** and will be upheld by the Court unless the challenger can make a "**clear showing** of arbitrariness and irrationality." This is the weakest standard of review and generally the government will win. As long as the government can successfully assert that the law has a rational basis or **legitimate government purpose**, the government will win.

OTHER STANDARDS OF REVIEW:

1. Rational Basis "Plus" (With a Bite): Although it isn't really used on the bar exam, some quasi-suspect classes, such as the mentally challenged and gay, lesbian, bi and transgender persons (this latter category has fluctuated, depending on the context), get rational basis scrutiny "with a bite." This means that the law under rational basis scrutiny can be struck down when there is a legitimate governmental purpose AND that the primary purpose of the law was not to discriminate against that particular class. See *Romer v. Evans*, where a law targeting homosexuals was struck down because the court found that the intent of the law was discriminatory.

Strict Scrutiny: The law is <u>necessarily</u> related to a <u>compelling</u> governmental interest.
Intermediate Scrutiny: The law is <u>substantially</u> related to an <u>important </u>governmental interest.
Rational: The law is <u>rationally</u> related to a <u>legitimate</u> governmental interest.

CRITICAL WRITING ESSAY (Property Law)

Oliver Owney owned an estate of approximately 350 acres outside of Greensboro. The tract was located in a hilly and picturesque area and was surrounded by trees, with the exception of the east side, which fronted a spring-fed lake. The north 5 acres had a large house on it, a guest quarters, and a stream running through it. The border on the west side of the property fronted a narrow, 50-yard forest, which divided the property from a housing development of big 5 and 6 bedroom homes, each on an acre of land. Alice Patterson lived in the neighborhood that abutted Owney's land on the west side.

In 1997, Alice began training for the New York Marathon. Because running on streets bothered her knees, Alice would jog on the outside 10 yards of the forest on Owney's property, through the trees. She sometimes cleared the trees on her jogging path and made the ground suitable for running. The views were spectacular, so in a place that was not easily seen from Owney's house or any nearby road, Alice installed a hammock between two trees for napping and just looking at the sky. She took naps infrequently. The hammock was a piece of canvas strung between two trees, with a mat underneath, an all-weather pillow, a wooden step, wooden guard-rails and branches partially covering the hammock, giving it an enclosed feeling. Once or twice a year, Alice even slept in the hammock overnight, just to see the beautiful night sky.

Oliver was strongly allergic to poison ivy, which grew in abundance in the forest. While he vaguely observed what Alice was doing during one of his daily walks, he shunned the forested areas of his property because of his allergy.

One day in 1999, Oliver's dog escaped from the house and headed to the back of the property where Alice's hammock was located. Oliver caught the dog right on the perimeter of his

219

property. Alice was heading toward the area at that exact moment, ready to take a jog. Oliver started talking with Alice, in full view of the hammock. He found out she was training for the marathon, smiled, and said, "Good luck." Oliver added, "Nice hammock; you just need a better roof," and turned to leave. As he was leaving, he yelled, "Just don't jog on my property; there's a lot of poison ivy on it." Alice ignored the warning and kept on jogging on Oliver's property. In 1999, Oliver began walking as exercise, and would use Alice's jogging path, but they didn't run into each other.

Alice exercised weekly through November 2005. At that time, Alice hurt her leg and stopped using "the track," as she called Owney's land. After her leg healed three months later, she started up again, even taking naps in the hammock. Soon after, Owney decided to sell his property and move to Florida. Owney realized he would have to do something about Alice first, so he filed an ejectment action in early 2006.

A) *What is the best argument Alice can advance in the lawsuit to permit her to continue using Owney's land? Briefly explain. (30 minutes)*

B) *Will Alice Likely Prevail? Why? (20 minutes)*

<u>Note</u>: Assume the statute of limitations for adverse possession, prescriptive easements and other prescriptive claims in the jurisdiction is 8 years by claim of right and 6 years by color of title.

ESSAY ANSWER
A) What are the best arguments Alice can advance in the lawsuit to permit her to continue using Owney's land? Briefly explain.

ALICE'S BEST ARGUMENTS: [SPOT TWO SEPARATE
LEGAL ISSUES]
> (1) Alice will claim an <u>easement by estoppel</u> to jog
> on the path BECAUSE .... [an easement by
> estoppel is better than a prescriptive easement
> because...]
> > AND
> (2) Alice will claim a <u>constructive trust</u> to keep
> using the hammock BECAUSE ... [A
> constructive trust argument is better than an
> easement because Alice will be claiming
> possession and not use.]

B) Will Alice likely prevail?

<u>Alice's Jogging Path Claims [50% of Essay]</u>

EASEMENT BY ESTOPPEL.

1. <u>Elements</u> – An easement by estoppel has three primary
   elements: (1) the Grantor gives the Grantee a license
   plus (2) a right to construct improvements in (3)
   reasonable reliance on the Grantor's conduct or
   statements.
2. <u>Application</u> –
   A. Here, Grantor Owney gave Grantee Alice a
      license because [facts]
   B. Here, Grantee Alice constructed [facts]
   C. Here, Alice will argue she reasonably relied on
      Owney's permission or acquiescence
      because....[facts]
3. Argument's Weakness: Even if a license existed, were
   the improvements made by Alice based on Owney's
   permission? Arguably no.

<u>Alice's Claim to the Hammock</u>

CONSTRUCTIVE TRUST

Alice will claim she has a constructive trust to continue using the hammock.

1. <u>Elements</u> - A constructive trust is the functional equivalent of an irrevocable license. It is an irrevocable tenancy requiring: (1) a license to possess; (2) a right to construct improvements, in (3) reasonable reliance on the Grantor's conduct or statements. .
2. <u>Application</u> -
   a. Here, there was a license to possess because [facts]
   b. Here, there was a right to construct improvements because [facts]
   c. Here, there was reasonable reliance by Alice on Owney's statements because [facts]

■■ı

WHERE STUDENTS GO WRONG IN WRITING

        a.   Not answering the question asked
        b.   Weak Organization
        c.   Taking Wrong Turns (missing the issues)
        d.   A lack of depth of knowledge
        e.   Execution/Application

Applying Your Knowledge

_____

_____

_____

_____

_____

_____

_____

_____

_____

_____

_____

_____

_____

_____

_____

The Workbook Chapter

_____

_____

_____

_____

_____

_____

_____

_____

_____

_____

_____

_____

_____

_____

_____

Applying Your Knowledge

_____

_____

_____

_____

_____

_____

_____

_____

_____

_____

_____

_____

_____

_____

_____

The Workbook Chapter

_____

_____

_____

_____

_____

_____

_____

_____

_____

_____

_____

_____

_____

_____

_____

Applying Your Knowledge

_____

_____

_____

_____

_____

_____

_____

_____

_____

_____

_____

_____

_____

_____

_____

_____

_____

_____

_____

_____

_____

_____

_____

_____

_____

_____

_____

_____

Applying Your Knowledge

_____

_____

_____

_____

_____

_____

_____

_____

_____

_____

_____

_____

_____

_____

_____